ROMANTICISM
AND THE
RISE OF HISTORY

Studies in
Intellectual and Cultural History

Michael Roth, Editor
Scripps College

Previously published

Anarchism
Richard D. Sonn

Darwinism
Peter J. Bowler

Dissent and Order in the Middle Ages: The Search
for Legitimate Authority
Jeffrey Burton Russell

The Emergence of the Social Sciences, 1642–1792
Richard Olson

Liberalism Old and New
J. G. Merquior

Renaissance Humanism
Donald Kelly

ROMANTICISM,
AND THE
RISE OF HISTORY

Stephen Bann
University of Kent

Twayne Publishers • New York
Maxwell Macmillan Canada • Toronto

Maxwell M   Sydney

Romanticism and the Rise of History

Stephen Bann

Twayne Publishers
Macmillan Publishing Company
866 Third Avenue
New York, New York 10022

Maxwell Macmillan Canada, Inc.
1200 Eglinton Avenue East
Suite 200
Don Mills, Ontario M3C 3N1

Library of Congress Cataloging-in-Publication Data

Bann, Stephen.
    Romanticism and the rise of history / Stephen Bann.
       p.   cm. — (Studies in intellectual and cultural history)
    Includes bibliographical references and index.
    ISBN 0-8057-8618-X. — ISBN 0-8057-8619-8 (pbk.)
    1. History—Philosophy. 2. Romanticism. I. Title. II. Series:
Twayne's studies in intellectual and cultural history.
D16.9.B355   1997
901—dc20
                                          94-12814
                                            CIP

10 9 8 7 6 5 4 3 2 1 (hc)
10 9 8 7 6 5 4 3 2 1 (pbk)

Printed in the United States of America.

Contents

Contents

Illustrations

1. Moreau le jeune, engraved illustration to Voltaire, *La Pucelle* (1785 edition), page 49.
2. John Leech, *Joan at the Walls of Paris*, woodcut illustration to A'Beckett, *Comic History of England* (1851–52), page 51.
3. John Leech, *Portrait of William Wallace, from an Old Wood Block*, woodcut illustration to A'Beckett, *Comic History of England* (1851–52), page 57.
4. Marie-Philippe Coupin de la Couperie, *Sully Showing His Grandson the Monument Containing the Heart of Henri IV at La Flèche* (Salon of 1819), Musée national du château de Pau, page 70.
5. Jacques-Louis David, *Death of Socrates* (1787), Metropolitan Museum of Art, New York, page 72.
6. Engraving of Strasbourg Cathedral (end of eighteenth century), page 86.
7. Effigy and inscribed tablet from the Faussett Pavilion (1769), reproduced from *Archaeologia Cantiana*, volume 66 (1953), page 92.
8. Effigy described as King Canute from the Faussett Pavilion (1769), Victoria and Albert Museum, London, page 93.
9. John Leech, *Canute Performing on His Favourite Instrument*, woodcut illustration to A'Beckett, *Comic History of England* (1851–52), page 95.
10. L. Sebbers, *Hegel in His Workroom* (1828), reproduced from a bulletin of the Hegel-Haus, Stuttgart, page 98.

Preface

In his "Inaugural Lecture on the Study of History," delivered in 1895, the British historian Lord Acton referred to the different intellectual influences that had contributed to "saturating the age with historical ways of thought . . . for which the depressing names historicism and historical-mindedness have been devised."[1] In these comments, Acton faithfully reflects both the general conviction that history had come of age in the nineteenth century and the nagging unease at a phenomenon that had become so widely and indiscriminately diffused. From his time onwards, historians have not ceased to refine and develop their methods. But their discomfiture with the cultural phenomenon of "historical-mindedness" has not, on the whole, diminished. It is difficult for the professional historian to come to terms with a general movement of thought that so blatantly transgresses the critical safeguards of the discipline.

This study is an attempt to run contrary to this tide. It takes for granted (and also seeks to some extent to explain) the prodigious interest in history in all its forms that characterized the period following the French Revolution. It also assumes an intimate connection (though not a connection that could be adequately theorized) between the new historical culture and the pervasive movement of Romanticism. Much of the material dealt with here will have a recognizable connection with what are generally held to be "Romantic" ideas and themes. But I have consistently tried to bring out the heterogeneity of the historical discourses that are brought into view;

and it is also assumed here that the "rise of history" takes it outside and beyond Romanticism as such, while remaining involved with the same essential problems.

Just as "Romanticism" will be given an operational meaning that accords with the nature of the analysis, so no attempt will be made to establish a specialized sense for the various cognate terms relating to history that will recur throughout these pages: historical-mindedness, historical consciousness, historical culture, etc. The ambiguity as to whether "history" should refer to the events of the past or to the representation of those events through narrative or other means is indeed one of the issues specifically considered at an early stage. But this is only because such an ambiguity became the subject of an interesting discussion within the period. For the most part, my use of such terms is nominalist, and presupposes that no "essential" meaning is waiting to be found.

The level of analysis will therefore not be that of general concepts; it will be confined to specific instances of historical representation and historical discourse (terms that I shall indeed seek to elucidate at some length). My contention is that the nineteenth century produced a wealth of insights into the cultural phenomenon of historical-mindedness. Hegel, Marx, and Nietzsche are just a few of the thinkers who looked at history from a metahistorical vantage point, and, in a real sense, our investigations have not proceeded very far beyond theirs. But, at the same time, little has been done to detach their concepts from the overall framework of each individual philosophy and to apply them to the specific analysis of historical representation. Marx's brilliant characterization of the historical role of Louis Napoleon in the *Eighteenth Brumaire* (1852) is well known. But what implications does it have for other instances of acting out history in "borrowed costumes"?

More recent influences on my approach will be no less apparent. Hayden White and Roland Barthes are acknowledged as pioneers in the field. My own study of the general phenomenon of historical representation in the nineteenth century dates back to 1970 and has given rise in particular to two books: *The Clothing of Clio* (1984) and *The Inventions of History* (1990). Although I am conscious that some of the material discussed here refers back to my earlier work, I should stress that it is complementary rather than repetitious. I have been particularly concerned to choose examples that I have not discussed before; or, in cases where some further reference seems unavoidable, to concentrate on an aspect that I had not previously seen as important (in the case of Du Sommerard's Musée de Cluny, I look especially at the specific issues raised by the description of Madame de Saint-Surin).

The decision to use predominantly visual examples is an option that will be explained extensively in the course of this study. It would, of course, have been possible to select literary texts, or historical narratives, for analysis in the way that White, Barthes, and a number of others have done. My choice of the image (which is never, of course, entirely divorced from a text) can be defended on a number of levels. Most obviously, a visual example provides a support for the exegesis that the reader (spectator) can also follow in a directly participatory way. Its very self-contained nature (as opposed to an extract from a text) enables it to generate cross-references as well as to provide a field for practical analysis.

My aim throughout, in fact, has been to provoke connections across the various chapter divisions: the historical image of Henri IV, for example, recurs in several contexts, and different aspects of the art of Bonington are discussed in relation to different concepts and themes. It is hard to know what a "representative" survey of the historical culture of Romanticism might amount to. Here the selection of one example rather than another—Bonington rather than Delacroix—can be justified not only for reasons of space but because one type of image may provoke more wide-ranging connections with the other images and contexts under review.

It will be obvious, almost from the start, that a high proportion of the examples are taken from French culture; on the other hand, the theoretical concepts used as a basis for much of the discussion derive ultimately from German thinkers. No doubt the reason for this bias is approximately the one Engels gave in his preface to the third German edition of the *Eighteenth Brumaire* for the "particular predilection" that Marx had shown for the "past history of France." France was, according to Marx's system, the country that most perfectly fulfilled the logic of "historical class struggles" and had emerged from its Revolution to establish the bourgeoisie "in a classical purity unequalled by any other European land."[2] Even those who are minimally concerned with Marx's class analysis can recognize that France, having generated and survived the Revolution, had a unique experience of historical discontinuity that was expressed, in a diversity of ways, through representation. If Germany and Britain were the forerunners of Romanticism, France developed the Romantic cult of history with an unequalled degree of clarity and explicitness, making it possible to gauge the importance of the stakes involved.

♦

I am happy to acknowledge the assistance of many people who have helped me to locate and acquire illustrations, in particular, Marie-Pascale Bault of the Maison Pierre Loti at Rochefort-sur-Mer; Paul Mironneau of the Musée national du Château de Pau; Rosalind Freeman of the National Museum of Wales; and Stephen Coppel of the Print Room of the British Museum. Jim Styles and John West of the Photographic Service of the Templeman Library, University of Kent, prepared prints from material in my own possession. Finally, I am grateful to Michael Roth for having negotiated a contribution to his series that incorporates an unusually large number of images and that gives an unusually close attention to them.

Part 1

The Context
of Historical-Mindedness

1

Romanticism and
the Desire for History

Romanticism was not simply a movement, but the movement to end all movements. So at least it can be seen from a perspective of two centuries on. For the ferment that spread throughout Europe from the late eighteenth century onwards, and reached its peak in most countries in the two decades following the final defeat of Napoleon in 1815, cannot easily be interpreted according to a specific agenda. A recent anthology, *Romanticism in National Context*, confesses from the start that there is "something intrinsically and astonishingly complex about Romanticism."[1] It is not possible to reduce it to a set of guiding principles, arising in particular social circumstances, as we might plausibly do for preceding great movements of thought like the Reformation and the Enlightenment. Hence one plausible strategy is to fragment Romanticism: to investigate the movement in its national context, given that the very concept of the "nation" derived its unique and continuing impetus from the political and poetic loading that it acquired at that time.

Yet there is an alternative strategy. Rather than looking at each national community for a distinctive cross-section of the concerns that animated the whole cultural domain, we can select a particular thread that traverses the entire movement. What I call the "rise of history" is such a thread. No one has ever doubted that one of the most potent causes, and one of the most widespread effects, of

Romanticism was a remarkable enhancement of the consciousness of history. From being a literary genre whose "borders" were open to other forms of literature,[2] history became over half a century or so the paradigmatic form of knowledge to which all others aspired. The "historical novel" set the pace for the novelists of the 1820s; the "historical genre" (*genre historique*) forced its way into the traditional modes of painting at the same time and remained there for half a century. Not content with invading and assimilating traditional media, the representation of history became the practice of new, intense modes of popular spectacle like the diorama and new types of educational display like the historical museum. Of course, history in the strict sense—that is, the history researched and written by an increasingly self-conscious cast of professional historians—was not divorced from this pluralizing and popularizing tendency. It tried, often successfully, to maintain its scientific distance. But this did not stop it being validated, in social and cultural terms, by the very proliferation of historical awareness that was fostered by the new, transgressive genres.

This is, as I have said, one thread in the multicolored skein of Romanticism. But there is good reason to argue that, from our own end-of-century perspective, it is the most significant of all. Much has been written about the collapse, over the last few decades, of the ideology of Modernism, which like Romanticism before it was a pervasive cultural movement involving every aspect of social, political, and intellectual life. This is not the place to comment on the various attempts to formulate a compelling definition of "Postmodernism," which would effectively describe the eclectic and diverse tendencies of the present day. But one point is obvious. To the extent that Modernism has receded as a cultural paradigm, it has inevitably brought back into view the lineaments of Romanticism, which now appear uncomfortably plain to us once again. The progressive and internationalist ideology of Modernism can hardly survive an epoch that, in Europe at any rate, makes us witnesses to the gradual disintegration of cultural identity into its component parts. We seem to be living through once again (though in vastly changed circumstances) the shock of new nationhood emerging from the supranational groupings that marked the experience of contemporaries of the French Revolution and the Napoleonic invasions. In other words, we can grasp the Romantic experience in a way that was inconceivable when the Modern paradigm was still in place.

This new proximity to Romanticism has been manifested in particular by a spate of intellectual and critical tendencies that bear precisely on the Romantic cult of history. A literary scholar like Harold Bloom has argued for some years that the modernist epoch was but the flowering of a vigorous late Romanticism, which itself established connections with the deepest levels of Western religion and philosophy.[3] A whole movement of scholars, drawing on new developments in literature, history, and anthropology, has been grouped more or less successfully around the banner of the "New Historicism," thus advertising a reaction against the prevalence of formalist and structuralist theory in the 1960s and 1970s.[4] To this very brief roundup of Neoromantic and neohistoricist tendencies, we might add the well-publicized debate that has arisen over Francis Fukuyama's thesis of the "End of History."[5] It can easily be appreciated that a debate about the end of history, far from suspending interest in the historical estimate of events, in fact intensifies concern with this rare and distinctive property of the Western mind.

An even more widespread phenomenon should be noted here. This is the fascination, which is no less evident in Australasia and America than in Europe, with the conservation and re-creation of the historical milieu.[6] Some commentators take it as a condemnation of our society that architects and planners can rarely assume the liberty to create ex nihilo that was claimed by their predecessors of the Modern movement. And it is certainly true that a country like England, for example, appears to find it more difficult to balance the arguments between conservation of the old and creation of the new than does its near neighbor, France. But it would be foolish to take the proliferation of such "historicizing" tendencies—from the conservation group to the historical theme park—merely as a symptom of cultural regression. The collective consciousness that impels a community to choose a historical reconstruction, in preference to a new and functional design, is itself a product of a complex history and not merely a variety of false consciousness that we can afford to despise.

In fact, as I will argue, this historical consciousness is the product of the Romantic period, when the whole range of our contemporary concerns with the past first became accessible to representation. This was itself an aspect of a momentous social revolution, since for the first time historical data became meaningful not only to a small band of passionately committed "antiquarians" but to a mass reading public and, indeed, further afield than that. The great German art historian Alois Riegl claimed in his remarkable essay "The Modern Cult of Monuments" (1903) that the quality of "age-value" could be perceived by "people whose minds are otherwise exclusively preoccupied with the constant worries of material existence. The most simple-minded farmhand is able to distinguish an old belfry from a new one."[7] Yet Riegl would surely not have maintained that this was a matter of mere perceptual skill, divorced from epistemological considerations. If the "simple-minded farmhand" recognized an old building when he saw one, this was because the cultural distinction between the value of age and the value of novelty had become entrenched even in the more peripheral members of society, with the result that the government itself felt obliged to have a policy on the matter. Riegl's own essay was in effect written as a preface "to the legislative proposal for the protection of historic monuments in the lands of the Austro-Hungarian Empire" (Riegl 1982, 3).

This study will not attempt to retrace the complex stages of cultural and social interaction whereby an Austro-Hungarian farmhand could have become aware of the value of age (or an Austrian art historian convinced of the fact that he held this knowledge). Such a project would necessitate an intricate pathway through the labyrinthine structures of the popular press and mass education in the nineteenth century. But what I claim to do is to indicate, however schematically, the range of historical representations that lay at the origin of this process of popular diffusion. It is to the Romantic period, in my view, that we can trace the emergence of this novel and irresistible capacity for multiplying and diversifying the representations of the past in such a way that a new code—or even a new language—was learned.

In what way does this aim conflict or coincide with other, previously established ways of considering the phenomenon of historical-mindedness within the movement of Romanticism? The essence of my approach lies in the hypothesis that the sense of history generated in the Romantic period was, so to speak, qualitatively as well as quantitatively different from what had gone before. It was not simply the case that more people came to share the passion for historical objects that had previously been confined to the antiquarian milieu, or that the antiquarians and historians immeasurably deepened their knowledge of history (though that was certainly the case). An irreversible shift had occurred, and history—from being a localized and specific practice within the cultural topology—became a flood that overrode all disciplinary barriers and, finally, when the barriers were no longer easy to perceive, became a substratum to almost every type of cultural activity. But it is easier to point to this phenomenon in a general way (as has often been done before) than it is to analyze it in specific terms.

For the purposes of my analysis, the notion that historical awareness formed a new code, or a new language, is an indispensable, if chancy, assumption. If Nature abhors a vacuum (as scientists used to say), History certainly abhors discontinuity. Every kind of argument is mobilized, particularly after the decline of Marxist thought, against the notion that history can be credibly analyzed in terms of discontinuous stages rather than as a continuous flow. Yet we do not have to accept the validity of the Marxist, or Hegelian, dialectic to argue that cultural development can be understood best in terms of discrete stages. The psychologist Jean Piaget, whose life was devoted to understanding the development of cognitive structures in the child, suggested that "the history of Western geometry," from Euclid onwards, exhibits certain striking parallels to the stages of the child's development.[8] It may, in other words, make sense to talk of the development of this particular intellectual tool as if the human race (or that part of it that was engaged with the Euclidian tradition) developed new capacities in the same perspicuous way as a growing child. But is there any evidence that the "historical sense" may have developed in this way?

Marx certainly thought something of the kind, but his views quite neatly invert the approach that will be followed here. In the famous opening passage to his *Eighteenth Brumaire*, he asserts the necessity, however temporary, of borrowing historical forms in order to confront the issues of the present:

> The tradition of all the dead generations weighs like a nightmare on the brain of the living. And just when they seem engaged in revolutionizing themselves and things, in creating something that has never yet existed, precisely in such periods of revolutionary crisis they anxiously conjure up the spirits of the past to their service and borrow from them names, battle cries and costumes in order to present the new scene of world history in this time-honoured disguise and this borrowed language. Thus Luther donned the mask

of the Apostle Paul, the Revolution of 1789 to 1814 draped itself alternately as the Roman republic and the Roman empire . . . In like manner a beginner who has learned a new language always translates it back into his mother tongue, but he has assimilated the spirit of the new language and can freely express himself in it only when he finds his way in it without recalling the old and forgets his native tongue in the use of the new. (*EB*, 10)

Marx takes for granted that history—that is, the repertoire of historical representations from all periods—forms a "mother tongue" in which the revolutionary may temporarily express his consciousness before finding a way into the new language that is appropriate to the new political society. But what if the "time-honoured disguise" and "borrowed language" were impossible to throw off? What if they formed, not merely for the revolutionary figure (whose specific case only prejudices the issue) but for the average citizen, a definitive cultural acquisition to be added to, rather than exchanged for, a modern form of consciousness? As we shall see at a later stage, figures at the end of the nineteenth century who were not revolutionary, and admittedly not average, did literally "don" historical personas and "drape" themselves in historical clothes; in our own period such a practice has been institutionalized on a very wide scale indeed. Are the American folk who dress themselves up for Colonial Williamsburg or Old Sturbridge Village trying to develop a new, revolutionary consciousness? Clearly not. But the issue of what precisely they are doing leads us right back to the Romantic epoch and not (I would argue) before.

To many historians who have turned their attention to the Romantic period, this point is unavoidable. But their way of dealing with it is radically different from the approach that will be followed here. One recent and justly celebrated study, *The Invention of Tradition*, displays in its very title the analytic distinction upon which its contributors have taken their stand. "Tradition" is, at least in the context of the early nineteenth century, the creation of a phony past, as when the formidable Augusta Waddington and her friends "evolved a homogenized national costume from the various Welsh peasant dresses, the most distinctive features of which were an enormous red cloak worn over an elegant petticoat and bedgown . . . and a very tall black beaver hat, in the style of Mother Goose."[9] "History," by contrast, is precisely the discipline that serves to unmask such fabrications. Through diligent inspection of the archives, it arrives at the rational and indubitable conclusion that things were not as we always took them to be: the Scottish kilt, for example, through which so many dreams of Highland ancestry have been egregiously expressed, was the invention of "an English Quaker from Lancashire, Thomas Rawlinson" (Hobsbawm and Ranger, 21).

What such studies reveal to us is both instructive and amusing. It is impossible to resist the force of the evidence, just as it is pardonable to revel in the unmasking of customs and practices that have been viewed so solemnly. But what this approach fails to encounter, as it celebrates the perspicuity of the ironic modern historian, is the sheer excess and extravagance of the Romantic investment in the past. This, too, is a historical phenomenon, and we cannot simply brush it aside as eighteenth-century rationalists used to dismiss as superstitious the medieval "Age of Faith." In the preface to his highly popular *Histoire des Ducs de Bourgogne* (1824–26), the French historian Prosper de Barante exclaimed on the distinctiveness of his own period: "Never has curiosity been applied more avidly to the knowledge of history."[10] It is not difficult to conclude that this widely noted "curiosity," this "avid" pursuit of historical knowledge, which Barante took to be a delayed reaction to the conditions of existence in the Napoleonic epoch, went far beyond the limited motive that the historian of the present day tries to discern there: the historian looks for an image that will correspond, however roughly, to our own estimate of the professional, scientifically aware practitioner and finds instead the multiple distortions and aggrandizements of a hall of mirrors.

The next chapter will be more closely concerned with the perceptions of the historical writers of the Romantic period and their equivocal relation to the wider historical culture of the times. It remains, however, to gloss Barante's "curiosity" and "avidity" for knowledge of the past in a way that acknowledges his sense of the distinctiveness of the Romantic period, while displacing the focus from wars and revolutions to the wider context of the conclusive transformation of habits of thought. In his study *The Order of Things* (*Les Mots et les choses*), Michel Foucault puts forward the hypothesis that the Western *episteme* (the structural matrix underlying all forms of knowledge) was decisively transformed at the outset of the nineteenth century and that the role of historical consciousness in this transformation was a crucial one. He suggests that "the lyrical halo which surrounded, at that epoch, the awareness of history, the lively curiosity for the documents and traces which time had left behind" was itself a reaction to a numbing sense of dispossession: "all this makes manifest on the surface the naked fact that man found himself to be devoid of history, but that he was already working on the rediscovery deep inside him . . . of a historicity which was bound essentially to himself."[11]

Foucault's proposition is dialectical, even if it is not Marxist. It envisages a deep historical perspective in which "man" was to lose his central position as the measure of all things, in which provinces of thought like natural history and the study of language would turn out to have their own separate genealogies and laws of development, dwarfing him in the process. In this context, "history" becomes a complex and necessary strategy of recuperation, a way of imaginatively recovering what the humanist tradition had been blithely willing to let pass. "History" is the relentless appropriation, by text, figure, and scenographic representation, of what is already irretrievably lost. It is an effect of camouflage, or perhaps, in Freud's sense, a work of mourning, which achieves the displacement of one type of dispossession (the loss of the centrality of "man") onto another (the loss, or absence, of the past).

What are the implications of this persuasive hypothesis for the treatment of historical representation in and after the Romantic epoch? I am reminded of the remarkable shift in the development of politics and psychology that occurs when St. Augustine tries to argue out the fundamental distinction between the City of this world (*Civitas Terrena*) and the City of God (*Civitas Dei*).[12] The essence of the matter, as he maintains, is that the two cities are produced by "two loves," the love of the things of this world and the love of God; in other words, it is not bricks and mortar (or the gold and jasper of the New Jerusalem) that makes such a city but the psychological disposition, the desire, of the individual human being. In an analogous way, we might turn our attention from "History," conceived as the objectified state of things past, or as the scientific practice of reconstituting them in an accurate and intelligible form, to the "desire for history"; this would be a form of "curiosity" conceivably explained by Foucault's propositions, but not for that reason explained away.[13] In the study that follows, the "desire for history" will serve as a constant presupposition to the prodigal display of new forms of historical representation: we may deduce its presence whenever we seek to understand its effects.

2

Understanding the Past

The Romantic period was not only an epoch in which the "desire for history" expressed itself in innumerable ways, in which the "curiosity" that was in earlier centuries the domain of the collector and connoisseur became the prerogative of a mass public. It was also, I intend to argue, the stage at which history became self-conscious, and to that extent established itself, at least potentially, as an autonomous vehicle for imaginative reflection. If we accept, even in general terms, the force of Foucault's argument about the reaction to being "devoid of history," this does not in any way diminish the cultural significance of the transformation that was taking place. We can indeed affirm about the rise of history in the nineteenth century that something was happening of no less significance than the "Expansion of Europe" or "Age of Discovery" associated with the Renaissance. In the earlier period, the globe became imaginatively as well as practically accessible, as a result of the journeys of the mariners across the oceans. In the Romantic period, what was opened up in time was a dimension hardly less real and concrete, though its access depended not on physical displacement but on imaginative reaction to the relics of the past.

Of course historians, and others, had thought about history before. They had sought to understand and validate their practice by grounding it within the social context of their times. But these attempts were made in spite of (or, perhaps we should say, because of) the lack of any general theory about the nature of history as an institution. Such a theory had to await the bold formulation provided by the German philosopher Georg Wilhelm Friedrich Hegel in the introduction to his lectures on *The Philosophy of History*, which took their final form in 1830–31. Hegel goes right to the heart of the matter by considering, in the first instance, the constitutive ambivalence of the term "history," which (in German as in English and other European languages) comprises both an evocation of the past in general and a description of the records made of it:

> In our language the term *History* unites the objective with the subjective side, and denotes quite as much the *historia rerum gestarum* [history of things done], as the *res gestae* themselves; on the other hand it comprehends not less what has *happened*, than the *narration* of what has happened. This union of the two meanings we must regard as of a higher order than mere outward accident; we must suppose historical narrations to have appeared contemporaneously with historical deeds and events. It is an internal vital principle common to both that produces them synchronously. Family memorials, patriarchal traditions, have an interest confined to the family and the clan. The uniform course of events which such a condition implies, is no subject of serious remembrance . . . it is the state which first presents subject-matter that is not only *adapted* to the prose of History, but involves the production of such history in the very progress of its own being.[1]

Of the philosophical consequences of Hegel's formulation, no account can be taken at this point, though I shall consider at a later stage some of the implications of this totalizing drive that yokes history to the development of reason and to the nation-state. What is immediately relevant to this argument is the particular sense of intellectual triumph we receive from Hegel's formulation, which locates it securely within the Romantic period. It is almost a sleight of hand that leads him from the "supposition" that historical narration appeared at the same time as historical deeds and events to the assertion of an "internal vital principle": the first statement seems dangerously close to a tautology, until we realize that the condition of historicity is precisely the passage from inferior forms of social organization to the creation of the state. But once that link is made, there is the germ of Hegel's grand scheme of historical development, leading up to the Prussian state of his own day. Hegel has established a system whereby the very nature of history is to participate in, and make explicit, the self-realization of the modern state whose perfect fulfillment is the work of his own period and his own fellow citizens.

Obviously this supreme consciousness of the nature of history, and its ultimate purpose, was not restricted exclusively to those who had experienced the exhilarating rise of Prussia to a leading position among the kingdoms of Germany, ready indeed to wrest the mantle of Empire from the declining supranational state of Austria-Hungary. It is still possible to glimpse the same assurance about the possibility of comprehending and mastering the forces of history in the writings of a very different figure from the last decade of the nineteenth century. The English historian Lord Acton, convinced as he was that Romanticism had succeeded in bringing "into action the whole inheritance of man . . . *for the first time*,"[2] was able to trace a clear connection between the immanent movement of history towards a progressively greater measure of liberty and the role of the historian, who both contributed to and comprehended this process. For him, the decisive early sign of the change that had come about in his own century was to be detected in the period of the Renaissance. "It was then that History as we understand it began to be understood, and the illustrious dynasty of scholars arose to whom we still look both for method and material" (*LMH*, 20). But the final coincidence between the historical process and the knowledge of the historian comes only at the late stage that was Acton's own, as a prospective writer of the history of liberty: "And it is by the combined efforts of the weak, made under compulsion, to resist the reign of force and constant wrong, that, in the rapid change but slow progress of four hundred years, liberty has been preserved, and secured, and extended, and finally understood" (*LMH*, 60).

What Hegel emphasizes as a philosopher and citizen, Acton reiterates in a different key, and as a historian. But it is in the light of Hegel's trenchant formulations that we can best come to terms with Acton's very different political message. To "understand" history is for Acton very much more than to undertake the detailed study of one portion or another of the limitless extent of time past. It is to understand both a localized phenomenon and an immanent tendency, and the act of understanding is distinctively, from the Renaissance onwards, the appropriate activity of the historian.

When Acton notes that liberty has been "preserved, and secured, and extended," he attributes the successful feat to the "combined efforts of the weak" over the ages. But when he concludes that "liberty has been . . . finally understood," he draws attention to the vital role of the historian in consolidating the whole process. Liberty can only mean liberty understood historically. Historical understanding is what binds past and present together in an existential knot.

Is this what Albertine de Broglie meant when in 1825 she wrote in a letter to the historian Prosper de Barante, "History is the Muse of our time; we are, I think, the first who have understood the past . . ."?[3] Clearly the Duchesse de Broglie—the wife of a liberal peer and politician and the daughter of the celebrated Mme. de Stäel—does not scan the centuries with Hegel's eagle-eye perspective; nor does she have the advantage of Acton's end-of-century view of the period that has brought the professional historian into a position of unprecedented prominence and influence. Like her friend Barante (in the passage already quoted), she attributes the special understanding she and her contemporaries have of the past to their common experience of the turbulent years of the Napoleonic epoch, as a result of which all contemporary experience of history appears to be flat and unengaging. She concludes the phrase already cited by admitting, "and that is largely the result of the fact that our own impressions are not strong enough." For the woman whose grandfather, the financier Necker, had played a pivotal role in the early stages of the French Revolution, and whose mother had pursued a dramatic, if dangerous, sparring match with the Emperor himself, this sense of deflation was only to be expected.

Nonetheless, Albertine de Broglie is drawing attention not simply to a postimperial depression but to a contemporary cult. If "History is the Muse of our time," this means that Clio, at least, is active in the Europe of the 1820s: she is stirring up a frenzy of activity, even if it is in some sense a surrogate for the age that has passed. Here at least we can set up a basis of comparison between this perceptive, but casual, analysis of the contemporary scene and the more elevated viewpoints of Hegel and Acton. Hegel, the philosopher of history, directs attention to the fact that history has a written form: it is essentially a narration, as well as being a general designation of all that has taken place in the past. But the fact that this narration must be compiled by a particular person, the historian, is necessarily glossed over by Hegel, who wants to convey the mysterious truth that "the state presents subject-matter . . . *adapted* to the prose of History." In such circumstances, the historian can only appear as a kind of medium, interpreting to the contemporary world the promptings of the inscrutable spirit that is in the state. This is a different role from the hard but practical service to the muse of history that Mme de Broglie envisages.

In a similar way, Acton's achievement presents a perplexing aspect to anyone who wishes to scrutinize further the grounds for the "understanding" that he so prizes. For the great history of liberty that he planned to write, and for which the *Lectures on Modern History* could be considered mere jottings, never did get written. Acton therefore appears as the refined historical consciousness that has assimilated all the diligent research of the century—and particularly that of the "German school" inaugurated by Leopold von Ranke—and can vouch for the fact that the lesson of liberty, pursued throughout the ages, has finally been "understood." His awareness indeed soars above the degree of enlightenment that can be expected of one historian, and his later years are taken up with the planning of a vast collective historical project, the Cambridge Modern History, which will be the definitive and unsurpassable record of the modern world in its intricate and many-sided development: hence the production after which all historians can finally lay down their pens and rest from the frenetic labors of the nineteenth century.

Both Hegel and Acton, in their different ways, demonstrate the colossal ambitions of nineteenth-century historical-mindedness and, equally, the bizarre corollary of their claims to understand the past. Albertine de Broglie, drawing attention to the prestige of the new muse, suggests a more modest, practicable agenda. For if Clio, the muse of history, has become the muse of the Romantic epoch, then she has inevitably taken over, or at least dressed in her own apparel, some of the other muses: her distinctive subject matter can be disseminated through poetry, theater, and the visual arts, as well as through her chosen medium of the narrative history. It is this extraordinary irradiation of the whole sphere of cultural production by the prestige of Clio that I hope to trace in this study. An inevitable consequence is that, whereas for Hegel and Acton the message of history could entirely take leave of a material form and emanate from a spiritual world, my own concern will be with the way in which historical data enter the material world of representation. By definition, they find expression according to the laws of the media in which they are contained.

This is not an entirely new agenda. But it is still original enough to require some methodological preparation before the concrete instances can be introduced. Much has been written about the types of philosophical understanding to which the works of Hegel and Acton each testify. Comparatively little has been written about historical representation, and the second part of this study will be devoted to a general survey of the important operational concepts that have been developed in this field, with special reference to recent writers like Roland Barthes and Hayden White. But first of all, it is necessary to touch upon the issues that did engender passionate debate in the early nineteenth century: issues of historical method, involving the boundary line between history and fiction, and thus touching inevitably on the problems of representation. Once again, it is possible to extract from the general debate attitudes that are specially germane to the approach that will be followed here.

3

Historians on History and Fiction

In the period following the fall of Napoleon, history and historians began to affirm a cultural presence in Europe that was unprecedented. Yet the form that historical writing took, and the form that the historical profession began to adopt at the same time, was by no means identical within the three major national cultures featured in this study: those of Britain, Germany, and France. What I intend to do in this chapter, as a preliminary to a broad definition of the concepts of historical representation, is to emphasize this diversity, but at the same time to bring out certain of the common features of the ideology that developed during these years. It is, perhaps, surprising that historians who differed considerably as regards their social and professional status should have had so much in common. But this is no doubt an index of their common cultural participation in the European phenomenon of Romanticism and of their different stakes in the crucial historical experience of the French Revolution and Empire.

Britain stood apart from continental Europe in this respect, both as a country where the Romantic spirit had declared itself before the beginning of the century and as one whose frontiers had remained intact while Europe was traversed by the French armies. It is therefore understandable that British historians were slow to manifest the significant changes in status and attitude that marked the continental nations (and especially Germany). The great eighteenth-century historian of the Roman world, Edward Gibbon, was a man of letters who had imbibed the philosophy of the French Enlightenment and who made no secret of his contempt for the decayed culture of the ancient English universities. Indeed, he wrote his resounding *Vindication* (1779) in response to the peevish criticisms of clerical gentlemen based in the universities, whose ulterior motive in attacking the author of the *Decline and Fall of the Roman Empire* (1776) was the advancement of their own careers. Even as late as the middle of the nineteenth century, the intellectual prestige of history in British culture was still dependent on the independent status of writers like Thomas Carlyle and Thomas Babington Macaulay, who followed the tradition of Gibbon in adopting no professional affiliations. Carlyle's extraordinary work, *The French Revolution* (1837), was so personal in tone that it could scarcely inspire disciples or imitators. Macaulay's intemperate *Essays* (1825–44) on historical matters, and even his great project, *The History of England* (1848), were saturated with political dogma and treated contemptuously the notion of disinterested historical research. When the professional historians did begin to emerge in Britain—largely as a result of reforms in the Public Record Office, and not initially in the universities—there was little to be learned from examples such as these.[1]

By contrast, Germany was (as Acton fully recognized) the forcing ground for the new, professionalized historiography. And although we are now less confident than Acton in assigning a unique initiatory role in this process to Leopold von Ranke, there is little doubt that he symbolizes better than anyone else the profound change awaiting historical scholarship in the course of the century. His *Latin and Teutonic Nations*, first published in 1824, defined in its preface the new critical principles—with an overriding emphasis on primary sources—which were to be the hallmark of his many successors in Germany and the rest of Europe. There is no special reason why an independent scholar, working outside the academic community, should not have achieved the same high critical standards as Ranke, once the model had been widely appreciated and disseminated. But it is important to realize that Ranke did not simply publish histories; he set up, in the seminar system, a new medium for the refinement and development of basic historical research within the academic community. If Acton could, by the end of the century, contemplate a history by many hands that would extract the definitive message from the newly opened archives, this was precisely because he could already gauge the effect of Ranke's teaching on generations of historians both inside, and increasingly out-side, the borders of Germany. In the British and what might be called the Anglo-American tradi-tion of historiography, the Rankean model of good professional practice has been overwhelmingly influential. Nevertheless, if we are concerned not so much with a professional code as with the breadth and significance of historical representation in the Romantic period, it is worth looking with special attention at the French cul-tural milieu. Here the sharp contrasts we traced between Britain and Germany do not really apply. France had popular, individualistic writers of history, as well as a significant degree of professionaliza-tion. The gap between the amateur and the professional was not an unbridgeable one, however; indeed it often appeared to close over completely. Jules Michelet, who is without doubt the greatest French historian of the first half of the century, has been acclaimed not so much as a pioneer of historical writing as of the contemporary "human sciences."[2] This he may well be. But there is no doubt that Michelet was also a scholar intimately familiar with the new skills of evaluating and interpreting documents, even if he chose, by deliberate policy, to set the seal of his own individuality upon his historical discourse. Why this stance may be significant, in terms of the present study, will be explored in my later discussion of the polarity between history and discourse.

Prior to Michelet, and indeed in immediate contemporaneity with Ranke, the French historian Prosper de Barante presents an interest-ing case of the practitioner who, in a certain sense, overrides the strict separation of amateur and professional, and therefore presents a particularly acute diagnosis of the phenomenon of historical-mind-edness and its multiple cultural significance. Barante, who was born to a family of *noblesse de robe* in Auvergne in 1782, had a precocious but short-lived career in the imperial service, rising to the position of prefect of the populous department of Loire-inférieure by the end of the Empire, and shifting his allegiance to the constitutional monarchy of the returning Bourbons after the Restoration. The de-cline in the parliamentary fortunes of the liberal center party after the assassination of the Duc de Berry in 1820 left him with little enthusiasm for politics, and in 1824 he shot to fame as a historian with his publication of the first volumes of his *Histoire des Ducs de Bourgogne*. Barante's historical style, with its sedulous concentration on narrative and its deliberate excision of any element of nineteenth-century judgment or commentary, represents as clear and explicit a commitment to a specific procedure as that of Ranke's *Latin and Teutonic Nations*. But what in Ranke's case is presented above all as a cognitive decision—a procedure for ensuring the correspondence of his narrative to historical truth—is in Barante shown to be a stylistic as well as a cognitive option, one dependent moreover on a particular way of characterizing the historian's relationship to historical culture in general.

This is not, however, to minimize what appear to be quite striking correspondences between the two 1824 prefaces compiled by these two historians who had certainly no means of knowing each other's work. Ranke asserts, in a passage that has become famous: "To history has been assigned the office of judging the past, of instructing the present for the benefit of future ages. To such high offices this work does not aspire: It wants only to show what actually happened (*wie es eigentlich gewesen*)."[3] Barante's tone is different, eschewing the false modesty in favor of a concentration on the disposition of the audience, and more than hinting at a political connotation in his stress of the "impartiality" of the imagination:

> We are sick of seeing history like a tame hired sophist lend herself to every proof that people want to draw from her. What we want of her is the facts. In the same way as we observe in its details and movements the great drama in which we are all actors and witnesses, so we want to get to know what existence held for peoples and individuals before our times. We insist that they should be summoned up and brought living before our eyes: each of us will then draw the conclusion that seems good to him, or even will have no thought of drawing any precise conclusion. For there is nothing as impartial as the imagination: it has no need to come to conclusions; it only requires a picture of the truth to be retraced before it. (*HDB*, xxiv–xxv)

Ranke's dictum has, of course, been interpreted in conjunction with the principle of the concentration on original sources laid out immediately after his commitment to "*wie es eigentlich gewesen.*" But it has all too often been assumed that in vaulting from an issue of representation—*how* it actually happened—to one of research procedure, Ranke managed to englobe the former within the latter: in other words, he implied that to "show how it actually happened" was a function of the procedure of utilizing original sources, and not of his own skill as a narrator. Barante is more open about his method and his expectations. The epigraph to his history is a phrase from the Latin rhetorician Quintilian: "scribitur ad narrandum, non ad probandum" (the purpose of writing is to narrate and not to prove). What is advocated is therefore a specific literary procedure, which will exercise a particular effect on the "imagination" of the audience—conditioned as it will be by the still vivid experience of the recent historical period.

Barante's more open formulation does not make him a better historian than Ranke. By any objective test, he was a far less competent technician, and the popular appeal of his work in any case lasted hardly more than a generation. But this is immaterial beside the fact that Barante well understood the nascent challenge to historiography offered by the Romantic epoch. He overtly uses metaphors from other modes of representation: we are "actors" in a "great drama," and we require "a picture of the truth to be retraced" before us. But this provokes the obvious objection. Does the truth of history reside in the form of a drama, or a pictorial representation? If so, what is the historian doing in his self-imposed restriction to the medium of words? Of course, this is not a very strong objection, and it might indeed be called a trivial one. What Barante suggests is that "we" (the people alive at a particular time) use our "imagination" to conceptualize our relationship to history *as if it were* a dramatic representation: we also imagine what we cannot see *as if it were* a "picture." The resources of narration do not pale beside these vivid representational modes; it is the function of narrative precisely to exploit them.

Barante's model thus takes for granted what I have already called a "desire for history": as he puts it, *"we want to get to know* what existence held for peoples and individuals before our times." It is not a very substantial step to conclude that the "imagination" is animated by this *libido sciendi,* and that it is an active capacity to form scenographic and pictorial representations of the past that the historian (or at least, the Romantic historian) utilizes to complete the cycle of communication.

In drawing out this theme from Barante's sagacious preface to the *Ducs de Bourgogne,* I am not forgetting a manifest sign of theoretical difficulty (though not, I would argue, incoherence) that is to be found there. If he has no problem in conceiving of the historian's role as one of communicating with a specifically attuned audience, he is undoubtedly exercised by the borderline between fact and fiction and by the historian's duty to maintain it. He notes the tendency of contemporary historians to advertise too self-consciously their relation to their sources (in which case they risk becoming "érudits" instead of true historians) or to lose themselves in moral and political reflections: as a result of this neglect of the imagination, "the fictive heroes of epic, drama or novel, are often more alive in our eyes than the real personnages of history" (*HDB*, viii–ix).

This avowal of the inferiority of the conventional historian in a domain that, for Barante at least, is of the utmost importance acquires a note of contemporary urgency when he alludes to two recent examples of the fraying borderline between fiction and historical truth. The politician and man of letters Achille de Salvandy puts forward the view that "as we wished not only to learn, but to see and hear, the framework of a novel contained more truth than the plan of a history." Going further than this, the historian Léonard de Sismondi—already well-known for his work on the medieval period—turns "to a romantic fable to make us aware of the manners of an epoch which he [had] just written of" (*HDB*, xvii). In response to these two challenges, Barante's own position is entirely clear. Referring again to the classical precedent of Quintilian, he firmly underlines the point that the historian is not concerned, like the orator, with pleasing and persuading his audience as an end in itself: he has to respect the specific characteristic of the historical genre, which is the mode of narration. But this need not prevent him from competing with, and perhaps even beating, the novelist on his own ground. As he explains in a carefully argued passage:

> Charmed by the contemporary accounts, I believed that it was not impossible to reproduce the impressions that I had received from them and the meaning that I had found in them. I have tried to restore to history itself the attraction that the historical novel had borrowed from it. History should be, before all else, exact and serious; but it appeared to me that it could be at the same time true and lively. From these naive chronicles, from these original documents, I have tried to compose a consistent, complete, exact narration which would borrow from them the interest which makes them live, and supplement anything lacking in them. (*HDB*, xxvii)

It is fascinating to observe that the young Macaulay, in his essay "History," first published in 1828, recommends a not dissimilar attitude to the challenge posed by the historical novelist. But whereas Barante's purpose is to defend the new form of narrative history pioneered in the *Ducs de Bourgogne*, Macaulay (who at that stage had written no significant historical work) can develop a richly suggestive allegory for the impact on the historical world of Sir Walter Scott: beyond that, his confident assertion of the duty of the modern historian is a mere promissory note, due to be redeemed more than twenty years later when he began the publication of his *History of England*:

> At Lincoln Cathedral there is a beautiful painted window, which was made by an apprentice out of the pieces of glass which had been rejected by his master. It is so far superior to every other in the church that, according to the tradition, the vanquished artist killed himself from mortification. Sir Walter Scott, in the same manner, has used those fragments of truth which historians have scornfully thrown behind them in a manner which may well excite their envy. He has constructed out of their gleanings works which, even considered as histories, are scarcely less valuable than theirs. But a truly great historian would reclaim those materials which the novelist has appropriated . . . We should not then have to look for the wars and votes of the Puritans in Clarendon, and for their phraseology in Old Mortality; for one half of King James in Hume and for the other half in the Fortunes of Nigel. (Stern, 86–87)

Macaulay's resonant paragraph is shot through, like the other purple passages of his essay, with images that present an intentional element of incoherence, if not paradox. The story of the apprentice who surpasses his master is a familiar one, but it is given additional potency here by being set within the context of a medieval cathedral. How are we to take the analogy between the apprentice putting together a supremely beautiful window out of the "rejected" pieces, and the novelist capitalizing on those neglected "fragments of truth"? Obviously, it is Macaulay's sleight of hand that causes the analogy to cohere, precisely by displacing it onto the level of an already-achieved representation and, by eliminating the process of critical evaluation whereby the "fragment" of a historical source becomes a "truth." Ranke would not have made so seductive and yet so misleading an analogy in his 1824 preface. No stained-glass window comes to mind when we read his sober definition of the historian's task: "The strict presentation of the facts, contingent and unattractive though they may be, is undoubtedly the supreme law" (Stern, 57).

Yet Ranke himself undoubtedly registered the tremors induced in the world of historical writing by the novels of Scott. We learn from his first English translator that Ranke, only a few weeks before his death in 1886, was still regretting that Scott "was not more available for the purposes of a historian than he is."[4] The problem was, precisely, that Scott had failed to provide the necessary footnotes that would have enabled the indefatigable Ranke to check and no doubt incorporate his attractive material. "What valuable lessons were not to be drawn from facts to which the great English novelist had the key; yet, by reason of the fault to which I have referred, I have been unable to illustrate many of my assertions by reference to him" (Bann 1984, 30). Ranke's predicament enables us to detect the flaw in the young Macaulay's blithe assertion that the "truly great historian" would reclaim the materials appropriated by the novelist. For what the historian requires is not simply an attractive "fragment of truth" but the possibility of recovering the original source used by the intrusive amateur, and then subjecting it to the same rigorous process of critical evaluation as all of his other material. If the novelist does not play his game, he is powerless: his King James may update Clarendon, but it will have to leave Scott's *Fortunes of Nigel* virtually unscathed.

The rivalry between the historian and the novelist to which Barante and Macaulay drew attention in the 1820s was thus not settled to the advantage of either of the participant factions. In retrospect, the scenario by which the historian blithely "reclaims" the materials appropriated by the novelist appears both naive and optimistic. What is more than obvious is the fact that novelists and historians obeyed different protocols and different norms of professional practice, which meant that their writings had (and continue to have) quite different destinies. It is hardly an exaggeration to say that no one now reads the historical works of the nineteenth century: the high, indeed almost unassailable, status that Ranke acquired as the leader of the new professional historiography has led, with a certain logic, to the valuation of precisely that characteristic that doomed his successive works of history to obsolescence; what is valued is the critical evaluation of sources that generates a constant reappraisal, and rewriting, of history, whilst the notion of a definitive, unsurpassably full historical record cherished by Acton comes to seem no more than a mythic curiosity in the progress towards self-knowledge of the professional historian.

No one reads the histories of the nineteenth century. On the other hand, people have continued to read the historical novels produced by authors from Scott onwards, and it appears that they are increasingly drawn to look at other forms of historical representation that were generated at the height of the Romantic epoch and continued to exercise their power, in differing ways, throughout the century. Having set up this contrast in starkly opposed terms, I am impelled to modify it to some degree. As we shall see at a later stage, the histories of the nineteenth century *are* now beginning to be read, and the reason for reading them is not simply to acknowledge the mythic progenitors of a professional good conscience in which the modern historian takes pride. We have seen in this chapter that historians like Barante and Michelet were willing to concede that the historian should appeal to the "imagination" of the reader; willing (at least in Macaulay's case) to illustrate points about the aspirations of the new historian by plundering the seductive vocabulary of the visual arts. But they were not willing to relinquish—any more than Ranke was—the view that their practice was, in some essential way, distinctive and inimitable. It falls to us to look at the continuum of historical representation in which their works participated: this need not mean dissolving their specificity, but it does inevitably imply suspending the universal operation of the dichotomy between "truth" and "fiction." That dichotomy, at any rate, is the bluntest of instruments for analyzing the proliferation of new forms in which the historical understanding sought to express itself in the Romantic period.

Another way of presenting this significant change in emphasis would be to stress that there are two quite separate, though obviously interrelated, definitions of history with which we have to reckon at this stage—and up to the present day. One is intrinsic, and the other extrinsic. The intrinsic definition refers to the development of history as a professional, and increasingly scientific, discipline, which sets itself apart from the activity of amateurs, however well-meaning, and rejects the wider world of historical representation as simply unworthy of interest. The extrinsic definition refers to something that is more difficult to pin down, because it is precisely the inundation of literary, visual, and spectacular forms of expression with a historical tincture. Yet its very diffuseness does not prevent it from being, in itself, a historical phenomenon of the greatest importance; nor does it necessarily impede analysis, provided that we place the issues in a correct perspective.

Prosper de Barante, whose reputation as a professional historian scarcely survived his own lifetime, was himself more than usually attentive to this wider definition of history, which he correctly observed to be a social and cultural phenomenon of immense interest, indeed the characteristic mark of his own century. In the essay, "On History," which he originally wrote for an encyclopedia in 1828, he concluded by drawing attention to "this historical fever which has not yet produced all its effects."[5] His final paragraph is as revealing for what it excludes as for its perceptive comments on the arrival of what has been called "historicism":

> But what makes our own century eminently historical, is that in literary criticism, and in the moral and political sciences, it proceeds by the narration and examination of the past. Instead of judging, or blaming, or prescribing the imitation of models; instead of proposing new systems, the writers of the 19th century explain and comment on the works which have been left to us by the generations of yesteryear; they seek to discover what circumstances, what state of things exercised an influence on their ideas, on their opinions and on their taste. They enquire not so much into the errors and defects as into the causes which have rendered necessary these errors and defects. In all things it is progression which interests us. We seek in the past for motives which will give us confidence in the future and we wish to endow the historian with the high mission of the prophet. (*EHB*, 219)

Barante's analysis of his age comes unstuck, surely, at the very point where he tries a little lamely to switch horses in midstream; having noted the obsessive interest in the past, he suddenly tries to explain it as a passionate commitment to the future. This hardly carries conviction. Or at least it appears plausible only to the extent that we are willing to read into it an agenda comparable with the one advanced by Foucault (and already discussed here). According to the thesis that nineteenth-century man found himself "devoid of history" and needed to recover "a historicity . . . bound essentially to himself," it does indeed make sense to view historicism as a necessary strategy of recuperation, which will generate a "new confidence in the future." For Foucault, however, the "man" that is at the center of this vision remains an uneasy composite of the hopes and fears of the Romantic generation, reinforcing his uncertain sense of identity through a selective reading of the past.

It hardly needs saying that the Romantics did not see themselves in this way. In retrospect, it is their sanguine ability to paper over the cracks that strikes us as symptomatic rather than their insight into their own investment in history. But, before we pride ourselves on our superior viewpoint, we should recognize that it was precisely this intensified awareness of the need for history, and of man's stake in it, that was to give rise, ultimately, to the possibility of the demythologized interpretation advocated by Foucault and his followers. Admittedly, for the bourgeois historians of the Romantic epoch, as for their Marxist successors, the primary phenomenon of modern history was the upward and onward movement of the people: as Augustin Thierry expressed it in his history of the *Tiers Etat*, the "progress" of the "Third Estate" "resembles that of a rising tide, which seems to advance and recede without interruption, but which still gains ground and reaches its destined point."[6] Yet long before the end of the century, with the writings of Nietzsche in particular, it has become apparent that it is precisely the identity of this collective hero of history—eternal "man," or newly emerging "Third Estate"—that must be open to question.

Nietzsche indeed affords—and not for the last time in this study—the precious hints that will enable us to understand the development of historical consciousness from its Romantic base. Hegel proposed in his *Philosophy of History* (as has already been emphasized) the imaginative thesis that written history dates inevitably from the point at which there was historical material worthy of record, in other words, from the period of the foundation of the state. Nietzsche brilliantly turns this concept on its head, in his "Of First and Last Things," when he argues that "everything *essential* in the development of mankind took place in primeval times, long before the four thousand years we more or less know about."[7] In other words, the unstated effect of the history that Hegel celebrates is to enshrine at its center a model of "mankind" that is itself fundamentally unhistorical: from this concerted attempt to ignore "primeval times" springs the myth of man's centrality that the Romantic generation vainly attempted to preserve. Nietzsche has a warning for historians: "The whole of teleology is constructed by speaking of the man of the last four millennia as of an *eternal* man towards whom all things in the world have had a natural relationship from the time he began. But everything has become: there are *no eternal facts*, just as there are no absolute truths. Consequently what is needed from now on is *historical philosophizing*, and with it the virtue of modesty" (*HAH*, 13). As this passage suggests, Nietzsche fully understood that it was necessary not only to invert the message of Hegel but to dissolve the entity that lurked at the very heart of nineteenth-century historicism. It was necessary to break down the notion of "man" that gave historical-mindedness its vantage point, and indeed its raison d'être. In this respect, Foucault's radical thesis about the reaction to being "devoid of history" as the constitutive movement of historicism finds its direct ancestor.

But Nietzsche went further than this. In the long essay *The Use and Abuse of History*, published in 1873, he engaged in a uniquely powerful meditation on the historical culture of the nineteenth century whose implications are still very far from being exhausted. I have already suggested that it is important to reflect on the way in which "the desire for history" characterizing this period preexisted, and produced, a remarkable series of concrete effects. Nietzsche not only takes this for granted; he actually breaks down the general notion of the "necessity" of history into three separate "relations," each of which is a vital component of historical consciousness. "History," he explains, "is necessary to the living man in three ways: in relation to his action and struggle, his conservatism and reverence, his suffering and his desire for deliverance. These three relations answer to the three kinds of history—so far as they can be distinguished—the *monumental*, the *antiquarian*, and the *critical*."[8]

This insight is precious precisely because it leads us out of the charmed circle of historians reflecting on history, which limits the subject matter of this chapter. For Nietzsche is not concerned specifically with the historian's relationship to history—one in which considerations of good professional practice inevitably take pride of place—nor with the historical novelist's relationship to history—one the historian is bound to impugn, however dubiously his reservations may turn out to be grounded. He is concerned with "the living man," and hence with every conceivable modality through which the "necessity" of history can find expression. Furthermore, the three different categories of relationship into which he chooses to split the overall concept of historical consciousness offer a guide to the material under investigation here, which has not by any means lost its validity. This can be tested further if we place them in the context of a more comprehensive definition of historical representation.

Part 2

———

History as Representation

4

The Contemporary Analysis
of History and Its Antecedents

This study depends implicitly, and often explicitly, on the significant enlargement of the debate about history and its uses in the nineteenth century, which has been opened up in the past twenty years or so. Albertine de Broglie believed those belonging to her generation were "the first who have understood the past." And I would contend that in the closing years of the twentieth century we are witnessing an unprecedented series of attempts to understand that understanding. The investigation has acquired a breadth and scope over the recent past that we can only wonder at, when we compare it with the modest studies produced on similar, but more restricted, subjects a few decades ago. David Lowenthal's *The Past Is a Foreign Country* (1985) is a rich repertoire of almost every conceivable use and manipulation of historical data for present purposes, which takes its stand upon a Nietzschean presupposition of the necessity of history for life. As Lowenthal puts it: "Awareness of the past is in myriad ways essential to our well-being."[1] His remarkable range of examples takes in the grotesque and the unashamedly nostalgic, but it also acknowledges the plastic power of the critical imagination in a fascinating section titled "Changing the Past."

A work of similar ambition, though utterly different subject matter, is Francis Haskell's *History and Its Images* (1993). Subtitled "Art and the Interpretation of the Past," this confronts the very specific question of the historian's assessment of the visual image as a source of evidence. Haskell goes back beyond the nineteenth century, and indeed beyond the Renaissance, in his magisterial survey of the way in which visual evidence has been compared with written evidence and in which the coherent visual systems of the museum and the illustrated book have been employed to give credence to a series of reinterpretations of the past. His work is exceptionally rich when it encounters the Romantic period, with such important phenomena as Alexandre Lenoir's Musée des Petits-Augustins and Jules Michelet's historiographical creation of the concept of the Renaissance taking pride of place.[2] Nevertheless, it is of little direct use to this study, since it evaluates this mass of evidence explicitly from the point of view of the professional historian: essentially, it is Ranke's distinction between primary and secondary sources, and the question of where visual data belong in relation to this crucial distinction, that pervades the critical discussion. Are images historical evidence, in an unmediated sense, or is their very directness a lure, which should lead the conscientious historian to make more than usually strenuous efforts at corroboration and verification? The question is an important one. But it touches only peripherally the issues raised here.

In fact, the area of discussion to which I hope to contribute has developed as a result of the innovative writings of two theorists in particular, who worked in parallel but not convergent ways: the American historian of ideas Hayden White and the French critic and semiotician Roland Barthes. White's most substantial contribution was the powerful study *Metahistory* (1973), whose subtitle, "The Historical Imagination in Nineteenth-Century Europe," betokened a hitherto inconceivable grouping of great historians of the period (Michelet, Ranke, Tocqueville, Burckhardt) with great philosophers of history (Hegel, Marx, Nietzsche, Croce). White's aim was to write at the same time "a *history* of historical consciousness in nineteenth-century Europe" and a "discussion of the *problem of historical knowledge*."[3] Both aims came together—as did the very different protocols of the historians and the philosophers of history—in the formulation of a "poetics of history": that is to say, a formal system determining the limited number of modes in which and through which the historical data could be shown to be represented.

It is not difficult to show that White's innovative method decisively breaks with earlier (and to some extent, continuing) ways of coming to terms with the "literary" aspect of the historian's work. A study like David Lewin's *History as Romantic Art* (1967), which is devoted to the great American historians of the nineteenth century, proposes that "history is one of the most difficult of literary forms," in which "some convincing way of portraying human character" and attention to narrative as "a coherent relationship among events" are both absolutely necessary.[4] It is hard to disagree with such a modest contention, which would, indeed, have been entirely acceptable to the critics of the eighteenth century, when "history" and "fiction" had no determinate borderline. But does this make the histories in question "Romantic art?" However sensitive and ingenious Lewin's commentaries may be, they subscribe in effect to the traditional view of "style" as a necessary embellishment: the "truth" of character and the "coherence" of narrative are given elsewhere, and it is the historian's function simply to express them through literary devices.

In an article originally published in 1975, Hayden White shows clearly why this traditional interpretation of style is inadequate. As he puts it, "the historical discourse can be broken down into two levels of meaning."

> The facts and their formal explanation or interpretation appear as the manifest or literal "surface" of the discourse, while the figurative language used to characterize the facts points to a deep-structural meaning. This latent meaning of an historical discourse consists of the generic story-type of which the facts themselves, arranged in a specific order and endowed with different weights, and the manifest form. We understand the specific story being told about the facts when we identify the generic story-type of which the particular story is an instantiation.[5]

To put it simply, we should not remain on the "surface" of the historical text, noting the local instances of "literary" excellence, but should appreciate how the figurative devices employed have a profound coherence, which is itself a major factor in our appreciation and understanding of the account. What are these "generic story-types"? In *Metahistory*, White contends that the modes of "emplotment" of the historical text in the nineteenth century are in effect the most recognizable and accessible of all, in fact precisely those utilized by the critic Northrop Frye for the description of genres of literature: those of "romance," "comedy," "tragedy," and "satire." To argue that Ranke emplotted his histories in the form of "comedy," whilst Tocqueville emplotted his work in the form of "tragedy," was therefore to make an overall judgment about the generic mode in which the historical message would be received: briefly, in Ranke, the conflicts of history pointed to an eventual state of reconciliation on earth (as in the final scene of a comedy), whilst for Tocqueville they were irreconcilable and took on a literally tragic dimension. But White also wanted to demonstrate how these overall generic classifications could be identified with a specific "poetics" in the construction of the historical discourse: the historian, or philosopher of history, employed tropes, or rhetorical devices, like metaphor, metonymy, synecdoche, and irony, in accordance with the generic mode that had been (consciously or unconsciously) selected.

As has been widely recognized, this program announced in *Metahistory* was not an end but a beginning. Rather than definitively settling the issues of historical representation in the nineteenth century, White's work opened up innumerable new ways of analyzing the texts that had, up to that point, remained essentially unread. Hence it is worth pointing out not the respects in which this study is indebted to him (which will in any case be clear) but the specific limitations of *Metahistory* and its associated essays as regards the concept of historical representation being advanced here. In the first place, White does not specifically address the question—which is crucial here—of the distinctiveness of the period initiated by the Romantic movement, as far as history is concerned. That is to say, he fully acknowledges the point that the nineteenth century was "history's golden age" and sees his work as preparatory to an attempt at the "reconstitution of history as a form of intellectual activity which is at once poetic, scientific, and philosophical" (White 1973, xii). But he advances no special theory about how this "golden age" came about. Indeed, his brilliant article on Michel Foucault, "Foucault Decoded," suggests that the notion of an epistemic shift from the "classic" age to that of the nineteenth century—the very notion underpinning Foucault's interpretation of the historicist mentality of the new century—is itself no more than a shuffling of tropes. Where Foucault sees the whole map of knowledge being redrawn, White finds no more and no less than a shift from metonymy to metaphor as the dominant figural mode in which knowledge (and knowledge of history among other forms) is represented (White 1978, 230–60).

In fact, it is plain that White does not seek to invalidate Foucault's thesis by drawing attention to its rhetorical underpinning, or "deep structure," any more than he invalidates his own text by undertaking a consciously ironic analysis of the previous theorist's aims. Far from rendering Foucault's basic concepts inoperative, he makes it possible to see how figural strategies like metonymy and metaphor can indeed be implicated in a broad theory of the shift in paradigms of knowledge such as Foucault proposes. My own work "Poetics of the Museum," dating from 1978 onwards, is centrally concerned with using the distinctions between tropes that White proposes here, not in order to dismiss Foucault's epistemological positions but in order to show how they can be related to the close analysis of distinctive forms of visual organization like the historical museum (Bann 1984, 77–92).

This mention of the historical museum relates to a further, inevitable limitation of *Metahistory*, which is its restriction to historiography and philosophy of history, among the many forms of textual representation. White produced perhaps his most decisive and iconoclastic move in arguing that the dominant figures who had been kept firmly apart in traditional academic studies, by virtue of the fact that they belonged to quite different areas of academic expertise, were both accessible to the same type of "deep-structural" analysis: like the lion and the lamb, Hegel and Ranke could lie down together in the metahistorical kingdom. But White did not venture into other forms: the historical novel, for example, or the myriad visual expressions in traditional media, and new, spectacular modes of presentation, which marked the Romantic epoch. Yet surely these were equally ripe for study? If the contemporaries of Ranke and Hegel could be credited with spotting "generic story-types" in historiography and philosophy, there was no reason at all why they should not be equally capable of doing so when they read the novels of Scott or visited the historical museums of Alexandre Lenoir and Alexandre du Sommerard.

This was an obvious, indeed almost too obvious, conclusion to be drawn. For in transferring White's categories of analysis from historiography and philosophy (where they had traditionally not been used) to historical fictions and systems of visual display, the metahistorian risked either falling into banality or making an assumption about the relation of word to image that was hazardous in the extreme. Scott's novels would not fail to yield up their "generic story-types," but no one had ever supposed that they were inaccessible to such analysis. On the other hand, the decision to analyze a historical museum, or a diorama, as if it were a narrative raised additional questions that could not be dealt with in such literary and rhetorical terms. In the eighteenth century, Gotthold Lessing's treatise *Laocoon* had argued strongly against the traditional critical practice of assuming that poetry and the plastic arts could and should reproduce the same data in their respective media: *ut pictura poesis* had been the slogan, but Lessing held that certain strategies were appropriate for an art of time, like poetry, and others for an art of space, like sculpture or painting. Surely the Romantic generation had learned the lesson, as critics and creators, that content—and historical content like any other form—cannot merely be transferred from one medium to another? Surely we too have to draw the same lesson?

It is here that the second major contemporary influence on the study of historical representation, Roland Barthes, comes to supplement White's contribution. Barthes was, of course, concerned with an infinite number of things besides the representation of the past: his writings touch on topics as various as fashion, photography, autobiography, drama, and oriental art, to name only a few. It is precisely because he took on this roving commission to look into these many spheres of human signifying activity that Barthes can provide invaluable hints about the analysis of representation as a continuum of cognate practices rather than a discontinuous field. Yet Barthes's contribution is, again for this reason, difficult to disentangle. It is split up among many disparate publications, themselves spread out across the course of a career in which Barthes's attitudes changed radically in a number of ways. Its most substantial feature is one essay, "The Discourse of History" (1967), which is flawed, though not seriously, by his determination to take an ideological stand on the future development of historiography.

This is the text that provides the most immediate and challenging comparison to the method of *Metahistory* (though it in no way serves as a direct influence and does not figure in the bibliography). White's avowedly formalist approach to the historical writings of the nineteenth century inevitably leaves out any consideration of the role of the author. This is not to say that he excludes any and every biographical context but that the historical text as such is envisaged as a repertoire of tropological effects, emplotted according to grand, dominant patterns like tragedy and comedy. Where is the author in all of this? Barthes, of course, does not reinstate the vulgar biographical author. But his very title, "The Discourse of History," advertises the fact that he is adopting an influential distinction made popular in modern linguistics by the French scholar Emil Benveniste. In determining the use of different tense structures in the French language, Benveniste formulates the distinction between two "planes of enunciation," which are those of "history" (*histoire*) and "discourse" (*discours*). Historical enunciation is the recounting of past events in which the speaker has no part to play. On the other hand, discourse is involved precisely when the speaker intervenes on the level of the statement. As Benveniste puts it, in the case of discourse, "every enunciation suppose a speaker and a listener, and in the former the intention of influencing the latter in some way or other."[6]

It might be thought that history—that is to say, a text about past events—formed the defining example of "history" as opposed to "discourse" in the linguistic sense. Yet Barthes deliberately takes the counterposition in his stimulating essay. He wants to ask, "under what conditions the classic historian is enabled—or authorized—himself to designate, in his discourse, the act by which he promulgates it."[7] In other words, he decides to look precisely at the signs (in Jakobson's sense, the "shifters") that mark the intervention of the historian in the historical text. He wants to examine not the history in its objectified, distanced form but the historian's act of communication, which can take the proportions of either a substantial preface (Michelet's preface to the *History of France* is the one cited) or a passing phrase (*as I have heard*, or *to my knowledge*).

The significance of Barthes's attention to history as discourse will be amplified and extended in the latter part of this study. In my view, such an emphasis provides an invaluable basis for analyzing the many nonliterary forms of representation that jostle for prominence in the early nineteenth century. For if a historical museum is not *histoire*—in the sense that it bears the distancing marks of the past sense—it is evidently a form of *discours*, to the extent that its founder and indefatigable guide himself assumes the role of interpreting it to the visitor. This approach will, of course, need much further development. For the present, it is important to stress that Barthes himself made no such connection. Indeed the general purpose of his 1967 essay is not to open up the nineteenth century to discourse analysis but to contrast the discursive habits of "classic" historians with the very different protocols of the nineteenth-century professional who "institute[s] narration as the privileged signifier of the real" (Barthes 1981, 18). In other words, what he holds as characteristic of the modern approach is precisely the suppression of the discursive dimension and the insistence that history is nothing but *histoire*.

Barthes is thus defending an ideological position reminiscent of his early preoccupation with the dramatic theories of Brecht, and with the oriental theater Brecht admired. Whereas in the Chinese theater a single flag can stand for a whole army, the culture of the West requires a plethora of unnecessary detail to endorse the reality of a scene. This devaluation of the individual signifier is also reflected in the nineteenth-century historian's determination to make narration the "privileged signifier of the real." For it implies that the material basis of the historian's craft—the conscious or unconscious choice of metaphorical and figurative language—should be subordinated to the mythic requirement: this is how it actually happened.

But perhaps the closing passage of Barthes's essay goes too far into the domain of wish fulfillment when it proclaims (with a confidence that we may well wish to associate with the fact that it was written before the events of May 1968): "Historian narration is dying because the sign of History is no longer the real, but the intelligible" (Barthes 1981, 18). From our own perspective, it is simply not possible to dismiss the lure of the real from the place it still holds in our historical culture. Indeed the whole conception of this book derives from the premise that the genealogy of the real still needs to be written—and that this is a matter of contemporary significance rather than a forgotten chapter in cultural history. The many-sided Romantic experience of history offers a skein of threads from which this genealogy can be teased out. This study follows a few of them.

If Barthes is too ready at this stage to dismiss the real as the privileged "sign of History," many of his other writings nonetheless demonstrate brilliantly the ways in which historical representation incorporates reality as a rhetorical effect. His early study of Michelet (first published in 1954 as *Michelet par lui-même*) testifies to his abiding fascination with the historian who used the conceit of the "portrait" to penetrate the corporeal being of his characters. In Barthes's eyes, Michelet's procedure as a historian is closely analogous to that of the painter: like the portraitist, he has to construct a particular frame for the historical action that is being accomplished. As he expresses it:

> The action "surprised" is in effect a necessary dimension to the representation of the human body in History. We see this in all historical painting, which is impossible without a certain solemnity. In Michelet, this posture is not decorative at all, as it is for instance in a painter of the Empire . . . what matters is that the man of History be presented in an amplified gesture, struck by an enchantment which transmits him through Time, neither living nor dead, in a third state of dreamed existence which enlarges and *imposes* him. However defective Michelet's Napoleon, he is of the same substance as the Napoleon of Baron Gros, for instance: both have that unreal fleshiness of the heroized man; their immobility *in front* of the historian or in front of the painter holds captive a *gestuary*, a style of action: History is founded.[8]

This is a highly suggestive passage; it is working throughout on the assumption not merely of an *analogy* between Michelet's "portrait" of Napoleon and that of the Romantic painter but of a deeper *identity*; what they hold in common is a "gestuary," or a repertoire of heroic gestures, which marks both types of representation as historical. If "History is founded," this happens as the realized product of a special kind of rhetorical effect (my discussion of the iconography of Joan of Arc, in the next chapter, will pursue this issue further).

Barthes's early interest in the representation of history finds its way into a number of intriguingly disparate channels: in his *Mythologies*, for example, he reflects on the degenerate historical "gestuary" of Joseph Mankiewicz's film *Julius Caesar* (1953), where the studio hairdresser has worked overtime to produce signs of Roman-ness in the straggling forelocks that stray across the conspirators' pates (see Bann 1984, 164–67). But his most challenging contribution comes from the repeated attention he has devoted to what might be called the cultural phenomenology of the "real." Here historical representation is not always the primary area of discussion. But history constantly finds its way in as a reminder of the excessive demands placed on the notion of the "real" in Western culture since the Romantic period. The past is, after all, absent by definition, and we can never bring it back. Yet, precisely because of its absence, it offers a particularly great imaginative challenge to the writer or visual artist who seeks to re-create its presence. The proliferation of different media, each striving to achieve the technical effect of presence more compellingly than its predececessor, is integrally linked to the desirability (and also impossibility) of historical re-creation.

As will be apparent at a later point in my argument, Barthes's most profound contribution to the study of this phenomenon comes in the course of his meditations on photography. These finally culminate in his very last book, *Camera Lucida* (*La Chambre claire*, 1980), where he considers "A Paradox: The Same Century Invented History and Photography" (Barthes 1981, 5). It may indeed appear paradoxical that historical consciousness, insofar as it is committed to "a purely intellectual discourse which abolishes mythic Time," should have a connection with the photograph, "a sure testimony, but a fleeting one." But Barthes well understands the profound symmetry between these distinctive "inventions." My own sortie into this territory will deal with the emergence of the conditions for the technical, yet also mythic procedure of the facsimile, whose connections with the altogether more spectacular regime of the photograph are obviously very close, though they need not detain us here.

What needs to be mentioned, however, is Barthes's second and substantial contribution to the analysis of historical representation: an essay published the year after "The Discourse of History" under the title "The Reality Effect." In this short but highly influential piece, historical narration (Michelet's description of the events leading up to the death of Charlotte Corday) is paired with the narration of the "realist" short story (Flaubert's "Un coeur simple"). It is explicitly assumed that the writer of fiction has followed on from the historian (and, specifically, the new professional historian of the early nineteenth century) in elaborating specific techniques for the recreation of the real:

> History . . . is in fact the model for those narratives which accept, as a filling for the gaps in their functions, *notations* which are structurally superfluous. It is logical, therefore, that realism in literature should have been, give or take a few decades, contemporaneous with the reign of "objective" history, to which should be added the present-day

development of techniques, activities, and institutions based on an endless need to authenticate the "real": photography (direct evidence of "what was there"), reportage, exhibitions of ancient objects (the success of the Tutankhamun show is a sufficient indication), tours to monuments and historical sites.[9]

With the virtuosity that was second nature to him, Barthes here sketches out a field of possible inquiry that is very much coincident with that of the present study. He lights upon the surprising possibility that what is "structurally superfluous," rather than what functions as an integral part of a strong narrative, may be precisely what guarantees the authenticity of the historical message and what sustains it when it has taken on the guise of realism, or metamorphosed into a photograph or a display of the relics of a long-dead Egyptian pharaoh. All of this comes out of the comparison of Flaubert's meticulous descriptive technique with the apparently superfluous detail that Michelet inserts when he describes the arrival of a portraitist in the cell of the condemned Charlotte Corday, shortly before the coming of the executioner: "after an hour and a half, someone knocked softly at a little door behind her" (Barthes 1982, 15).

Barthes is an invaluable guide to the intricacies of representation, and his comments on the functioning of the "reality effect" in historical discourse draw attention to a central paradox: that the claim of historical narrative to represent the real is dependent on the historian's creative use of the "superfluous" detail rather than on the skill and scrupulousness with which the evidence has been evaluated. Although the instances he selects are drawn from narrative texts, it is also obvious that his precepts serve as a guide to the analysis of the construction of the real through visual devices. Here, once again, it is a question of assessing the rhetorical structure of the image in order to discover the particular device through which the artist has infiltrated, within a particular medium and context, the message of the real.

Yet it is surely not necessary to accept, a quarter of a century after Barthes was writing these studies, the sharp polarization he establishes between the "real" and the 'intelligible." If in 1967 he maintained the view that history was on the way to eschewing "reality effects" and becoming a purely intellectual discourse, he would surely not have found any confirmation of this prediction as an accurate one in the ensuing years. Looking back at the historical representation of the early nineteenth century from the vantage point of the 1990s, we have even less justification for believing we have decisively parted company with the historical culture of Romanticism.

5

Metamorphoses of Joan of Arc

In the previously quoted passage on the representations of the Emperor Napoleon, Roland Barthes claimed to find a common feature in the historical text by Michelet and the portrait painting by the Baron Gros: both had in common "a gestuary, a style of action." It is my contention that the visual image can indeed (to use Barthes's phrase) effect the "founding" of history. That is to say, the image offers eloquent testimony of the degree to which the historical past was perceived in its concreteness: it is the immediate correlate to the imaginative re-creation of history as scene and milieu. But does this imply that any image can perform this role? By what criteria can we recognize the authenticity of the historical image? And in what way does the Romantic period enable judgments and discriminations of this type to be made?

This kind of question arises implicitly from Francis Haskell's treatment of the portrait in *History and Its Images*. Confronted by the fact that seventeenth-century representations of the legendary Frankish king, Pharamond, were totally inconsistent with one another, Haskell hazards the suggestion that the French public must have been "baffled" by this proliferation of alternative images: "Had their earliest king been pinched and anxious, with skin pressed tightly over his cheekbones and a vaguely Hapsburg jaw lightly covered with stubble, or had he worn an Oriental turban on his head with a small crown perched precariously at the back of it . . . Or had he been a tough, thickly moustached and bearded creature with prominent ears and ferocious eyes . . ." (Haskell, 53). Indeed, the features described are completely different and seem to indicate little but the desperate resourcefulness of the artists, who had no original records to help them. But what precisely are we to make of this difference?

In order to reach the conclusion that contemporaries would have been inclined to judge one representation rather than the other to be historically authentic (or both to be equally inauthentic), we have to presuppose that they had a firmly grounded concept of the historical authenticity of the visual image. We have to take for granted that they would have credited such historical personages with a specific bodily appearance, and moreover that they would have seen such an appearance as a legitimate and possible object of representation. But is it reasonable to assume this? As is well known, the orthography of proper names differed quite considerably from writer to writer (and indeed in the course of a single writer's manuscripts) during the early modern period: the various spellings of "Shakespeare" are a case in point. It would make no sense to envisage asking one of Shakespeare's contemporaries which was the "right" spelling of his name. The question is, therefore, whether the different images of Pharamond may not have been governed by the economy of a purely combinatory or rhetorical variation (as with the inconstant proper names) rather than being tied to a notion of singularity that implied a concrete vision of the remote historical milieu.

Of course, I am not claiming that the distribution of different features in a portrait image is directly analogous to the variation of letters in a written proper name. But the comparison seems to me valid nonetheless. Haskell's description of the portraits of Pharamond does indeed split them up into syntactic features: cheekbones and Hapsburg jaw, precariously perched turban, thick moustache, and ferocious eyes. In the way in which they are specified, it is possible to think of all of these characteristics being identifiable under the general category of "exotic and ferocious sovereign." But no specifically historical judgment of the plausibility of any one set of characteristics need be involved. It seems likely that the seventeenth-century spectators of Pharamond remained historically agnostic.

I cite this fascinating instance as a prelude to a different type of comparison between portrait images, one of which dates from shortly before, and the other from shortly after, the Romantic period. Both deal with the exploits of Joan of Arc. In an engraving by Moreau le jeune for the 1785 edition of Voltaire's play, *La Pucelle*, Joan is seen bearing down from the walls of Orleans onto the English commander, Talbot, who prepares to engage her in single combat. In a plate from Gilbert Abbott A'Beckett's *Comic History of England* (1851–52), by contrast, John Leech's woodcut presents her scaling the walls of Paris with a determined look on her face. She may not succeed in entering the city, but at least she has managed to tweak one of her English opponents quite forcefully by the nose!

Demonstrably these two representations of the Maid of Orleans derive from two different "generic story-types," as Hayden White might have put it. We do not need to search very far in order to recognize what these may be. Voltaire encodes the story of Joan of Arc specifically as a *romance*. In his verse drama, Joan, naked with sword in hand, delivers Agnes Sorel from the Benedictine convent where she has been held prisoner by the English; more decently arrayed, and perched upon her "holy ass," she then engages in single combat with the enemy commanders Talbot and Chandos; and finally, after more escapades and adventures, she yields her virtue to her love for her handsome companion in arms, Dunois.[1] Insofar as the story-type is that of a romance, Voltaire's version does indeed seem potentially transgressive, since the formidable Maid must act the part of the traditional male hero throughout most of the action, only to be recuperated as a heroine in the final turn of the drama. Earlier in the eighteenth century, Mme. Durand's *Mémoires de la Cour de Charles VII* (1737) had presented her as a lovely shepherdess, serenaded by the Sire de Baudricourt, who had disguised himself as a shepherd and brought along his lute for the purpose.

It may be impossible for us to view the "romance" of Joan of Arc in other than ironic terms. Still, it is important to bear in mind that our sense of the anomaly of portraying Joan of Arc as a swordswoman or a Rococo shepherdess is dependent on a prior notion of what the historical Joan might have been. How should we weigh the fact that the audience for which Voltaire and Mme. Durand were writing had no such notion? Equally, it is impossible for us not to notice that the Leech illustration to the significantly named *Comic History of England* is intended as satire: Leech himself, of course, was a prominent exponent of the satirical genre of caricature.[2] Should we therefore conclude that the unconscious irony of Moreau le jeune and the intentional caricature of Leech amount to the same thing and that neither of them is worth taking seriously as historical representation? Surely this would be to ignore the crucial point that follows on from our recognition that the audience of Voltaire and Mme. Durand had no historical referent to set against the more or less arbitrary conversion of Joan into a dashing swordswoman or a melting shepherdess? By 1850, the purchasers of A'Beckett's *Comic History of England* did indeed have such a referent; the satirical Joan of Leech's picture must therefore be measured against the accumulating knowledge of what the historical Joan might have been like.

This is a crucial point in my argument, and it must therefore be defended against the possible objection that I am simply asserting a difference, which the two images do not in any way corroborate or support. In order to do this effectively, it is necessary to broaden somewhat the context within which the individual images belong. Moreau le jeune's Joan derives, as is obvious, from a plate illustrating a particular juncture in Voltaire's play. According to convention, it quotes the relevant couplet as a caption: "In place of friends, Joan, with her lance in hand, / Bore down at him upon her holy ass." It is, undoubtedly, the strictness of the metric scheme that has given us the "holy ass" (*âne divin*) rather than a more conventional horse—and the artist has had some fun in reinterpreting Bellerophon, the mythological steed of Perseus, for this medieval rendezvous. Nevertheless, the main components of the image, and most significantly the costume, are taken not from the imagination but from the conventional repertoire of contemporary stagecraft. The English commander Talbot wears a plumed helmet and a dramatic sash that cuts across the burnished front of his breastplate. The plume would have been an inseparable accompaniment to a chivalric costume, even in such musical representations as Jean-Baptiste Lulli's production of *Armide* (1764); the actor La Rive played the Norman knight Tancred with a sash to denote the medieval provenance of his otherwise composite costume, while Lekain's appearance in the *Siège de Calais* (1765) anticipates almost all the finery of Talbot, even to the gauntlets (Lanson, 23, 30; plates III–V).

What we see in Moreau le jeune's etching is therefore a faithful reflection of conventions in costume and stagecraft that were, in the later eighteenth century, continuously evolving towards a more historically justifiable mode without ever attempting, or needing to attempt, what might be called "archaeological" accuracy. Obviously, the prime requirement for an actor or actress on the stage is

1. Joan of Arc on her holy ass: illustration to Voltaire, *La Pucelle* (1785).

to *signify* the ancient or the medieval world, the classical or chivalric hero; that signification is governed to some extent by what the public will accept as authentic (in other words, by the degree to which people can supply other tests for authenticity from their historical culture), but it is also governed by purely intrinsic considerations, like what will look good on stage and what will facilitate the action. Lekain may look smart and knightly in his costume, but no one will expect him to be wearing a real suit of armor.

The crucial difference with Leech's illustration is, in the first place, that the caricaturist makes no specific reference to theatrical models. Whereas Moreau le jeune has labored hard and long to create the decor of a rather pasteboard medieval town wall, Leech can suggest with a few careless lines the fortifications of Paris: the repertoire of examples the public is prepared to take as authentic indications of a medieval city wall has clearly been enriched over the intervening period by the representation of historical paintings, dioramas, even photographs, and signification no longer has to be routed through the confections of the stage. But this factor is itself bound up with a further, more pervasive distinction. Leech's illustration is literally part of a history book (albeit a "comic" one): it does not occupy a separate page (like Moreau le jeune's etching) but cuts into the text, like the many other inventive images Leech has interpolated, ranging from a mock historiated capital to a full-blown (and colored) etching on special paper. Its caption, "Joan at the Walls of Paris," is simply a relay that leads us back into the surrounding narrative; alternatively one could say that the narrative sets up the expectations that we then satisfy by taking a look at the cleverly contrived image.

In fact, the narrative of Joan's assault on the Faubourg St. Honoré of Paris is printed just above the image, and then breaks off to continue on the adjoining page:

> Joan threw herself against the wall, but could make no impression upon it; and she could only lament that among the French artillery there was no mortar to be brought to bear upon the bricks of the city. She then resorted to other steps—or rather to a ladder—and had reached every successive round amid successive rounds of applause from her followers, when she was stopped by a wound, which fairly knocked her over. A friendly ditch received the disabled Joan, who went into it with a splash, which caused all her

2. Joan tweaks an English nose: John Leech, illustration to the *Comic History of England* (1851–52).

companions to basely run away, lest they should participate in the consequences of her downfall. Drenched and dis-heartened, sobbing, and in a perfect sop, the Maid crawled out of the ditch. (A'Beckett, 258–59)

No "âne divin" is on hand to help Joan in this inconclusive skirmish, of which Leech has represented the second and most aggressive phase. But we must once again be wary of consigning Leech's im-age, and the text it closely accompanies, to the same epistemological space as the illustration to *La Pucelle*. A'Beckett's text is designedly "comic"; it signals its self-reflexive nature by the relentless punning that is a feature of the narrative: "steps" and "ladder," "sobbing" and "sop" create minor eddies of overdetermination in the flow of the story and remind us, if we needed to be so reminded, that this is not an action, but a story being told. But this self-reflexive ten-dency is dependent precisely on the preexistence of other narra-tives. One could say that A'Beckett's *Comic History of England* makes sense only in respect of its satirical—or, more exactly, parodic—relationship to the other histories which had begun to enter public circulation; not in relation to any particular history, no doubt, but in relation to the expectation that, in one or more such historical texts, a straight (rather than satirical) account of English history can be readily found.

This brings us to an important recognition that is perhaps implicit in Hayden White's "metahistorical" investigations, though it is not developed in any direct way. If we consider the different types of "generic story-type," or modes of "emplotment," to which the historical representation of the nineteenth century is subject, we are not merely looking at different stylistic options, which the author or artist is free to adapt in any way they please. We are looking at the development of a language in the broad sense; that is to say, a development of codes that themselves entail, or give rise to, the possibility of new codes. Here the already cited view of Piaget, about the parallel between the child's learning experience and the human race's acquisition of the discipline of geometry, is relevant. It may seem a trivial point that a "comic" or satirical history is possible only if there exists a prior conception of a "straight" history. But the point can be made more forcibly. Such parodic images as Leech's Joan of Arc are a faithful indication of a generalized histori-cal-mindedness that, involving as it did the acceptance of new and richly replete models for what could count as historical representation, developed apace in the Romantic epoch. Moreau le jeune's image belongs to a context in which historicity is no more than superfluous decor, while Leech's takes for granted the deeply embedded structures that the *Comic History* affirms in its very act of light-hearted transgression.

It could be argued at this point that I am taking for granted the existence of an entirely mythic construct: what could be called the grand narrative of history, authoritatively installed, against which all ironic or satirical departures have to be measured. Where was this narrative to be found? Clearly, it was to be found nowhere. But this does not mean that such a narrative did not have a kind of existence, as a Utopia, in the minds and intentions of historians. Both Barante and Ranke in their different ways hold to the view that the historian will be able to clear away the "sophistical" and "judgmental" aspects of eighteenth-century historiography and return to a faithful registration of the reality of the past. On the other hand, a slightly subsequent historian, like Michelet, is already aware that such an expectation of attaining what could be called the "zero degree" of historical representation is no more than a myth: the historian cannot efface the fact of living in the nineteenth century but must organize the narrative in such a way as to convey in the most dramatic fashion the consequences of having a "desire for history" while being forever barred from consummating it.[3]

Considered from this point of view, the parodic stance of A'Beckett's narrative, and Leech's image, seems less like a mere appendage to the serious commitment of the genuine historian and more like an indication of the intrinsic evolution of historical codes that historiography proper was also destined to experience. Let us return once again to Joan of Arc. Michelet published his three chapters on the life of Joan of Arc in the fifth volume of his *History of France*, which appeared in 1841, and in 1853 he made a separate edition of what had become a classic text in its own right. It was already well known in England by 1847, when Thomas de Quincey wrote a substantial essay on Joan of Arc and showed himself to be thoroughly familiar with Michelet's history. In what way does Michelet's Joan differ from A'Beckett's "drenched and disheartened" Maid? Obviously, a substantial allowance has to be made for the fact that on Joan of all people, English and French attitudes were bound to differ radically. De Quincey acknowledged as much when he lamented "the bitter and unfair spirit in which M. Michelet writes against England."[4] Certainly Michelet is not going to show Joan as, in any sense, a figure of fun. But it is nonetheless the case that his vivid, highly selective account of events does not mince matters about the inglorious situation in which the Maid had landed herself:

> It was indeed a foolhardy enterprise . . .
> The French, however, did carry one outer bulwark. The Maid went down to the first moat; she even cleared the saddle of earth which separated it from the second. Then she discovered that the latter, which surrounded the walls, was filled with water. Indifferent to the hail of arrows, she cried for faggots to be brought, while with her spear she was sounding the depth of the water. She was almost alone, a target for all the bolts; one hit her, and went through her thigh.[5]

This passage could not be mistaken for that of A'Beckett: for one thing, there is not a single pun! But it can surely be argued that the two passages by A' Beckett and Michelet each reflect a certain confidence in the capacity of narrative to espouse the accidents of history, combined with a distinctive self-consciousness about the author's attitude to the past. If we put it another way, Moreau le jeune's miraculous flying ass belongs to a world of theatrical contrivances and has no place in the company of a narrative that seeks to recover a complex but distant past. Leech's image not only belongs with A'Beckett's text, it is actually not far from the self-conscious revisionism of Michelet's medieval worldview, however satirical its purpose. Michelet began his chapters on Joan of Arc by insisting that, far from receiving assistance from flying asses, Joan of Arc was conspicuous for her avoidance of irrational strategies. "Joan's eminent originality was her common sense" (Michelet, 3). His demythologized Joan, as we can legitimately describe her, is a close cousin to the forthright young lady who tweaks the nose of the English defender.

It would take a study considerably longer than this book to trace the different stages through which Joan of Arc acquired a presence, both as the subject of a narrative and as the focus of innumerable visual images, in the period from the end of the eighteenth century to the beginning of the twentieth. Indeed Marina Warner has shown that, even if we confine ourselves to the United States, there is a rich tradition of evoking and personifying Joan. In its early stages, as with John Daly Burk's verse drama *Female Patriotism, or the Death of Joan of Arc* (1798), this appears to have as little relevance to "the historic Middle Ages" as Voltaire's *La Pucelle*. But there is a progressive enrichment, fueled by French historiography, as when Sarah M. Grimké, "the great campaigner for emancipation," produced an English version of the French writer Lamartine's biography in 1867. "The climax of adulation," according to Warner, comes when Joan's patriotic mission is used to reinforce the message of French national liberation during World War I and when Anna Hyatt Huntington's equestrian bronze of the Maid of Orleans is installed over the Hudson River in New York.[6]

There is indeed a fascinating story to be told (as Marina Warner's work attests) about the whole history of personification in Western art, which goes back as far as its remotest origins and obviously involves extremely complex issues of individual and collective identification. This is not our concern here. The purpose of introducing these two images of Joan is precisely to insist on a phase of that interminable sequence in which a distinctively new element is engendered: in brief, I am concerned not simply with personification but with historical personification—that is to say, with the possibility of lending a credible visual form to a person who is also known through an amalgam of historical and perhaps even fictional texts. In insisting that the admittedly parodic image of Leech's Joan fulfills this criterion, I am, however, inviting scepticism about the basis on which such a judgment can be made. What ultimately defines such a figure as historical in the eyes of the reading public? What kind of prior knowledge must be assumed in order for such a claim to make sense?

To answer these basic questions, even in a preliminary way, is crucial to the development of my concept of historical representation. It implies, moreover, returning briefly to the ideas that have been traced with reference to Barthes and White. White's view of the discourse of nineteenth-century historiography being governed by a repertoire of possible tropes and modes of emplotment helps us to understand how a satirical form like A'Beckett's *Comic History* is integrally related to the totality of possible forms of interpreting the past. On the other hand, Barthes prepares us for the recognition that the historical message, like any other message, is functionally determined by the possible means of representation: it exists in and through representation, and that implies a careful study of the specific media and conditions of display existing in a particular time and place. It is one of the significant things about A'Beckett's *Comic*

History that it not only indicates a sophisticated view of the different potentialities of historical narrative but also, in Leech's illustrations, displays the awareness that figural authenticity and historical representation are not one and the same. Leech's uproarious *Portrait of William Wallace, from an Old Wood Block*, conveys the important point that historical sources for portraiture reflect visual stereotypes (as well as the technical limitations of a specific medium): the "wooden" Wallace, festooned with as many badges of authentic Scottishness as he may appear to be, differs from the animated Joan precisely in the sense that she, unlike him, is empowered with a capability for action.

This enables us to see, at the same time, the importance in this connection of Barthes's helpful notion of the "reality effect." Barthes, we may recall, has two antithetical versions of how representation endorses the historically "real": on the one hand through the stereotype (the "action surprised"), and on the other through the bringing into prominence of the "structurally superfluous" detail (the soft knock on the door of Charlotte Corday's prison cell). Our two examples from Leech suggest that even in the form of a deliberate parody, this dual scale of possibilities is maintained, creating a kind of representational space in which the "reality effect," obviously, exerts the greater power on the imagination. William Wallace is indeed paralyzed in the impossible, frozen gesture that denotes his mock historicity. *Joan at the Walls of Paris* is, on the other hand, a scene of multiple actions and engagements in which we can, if we like, attend specifically to the superfluous detail that endorses the "reality" of the action: the unusual heftiness of Joan's sword, the firmness of her tweak, or even the sparring match between the two soldiers at opposite ends of the same spear all offer points on which the attention can fix, by contrast with the bland antithetical structure of Moreau's engraving.

◆

The implication that I wish to draw from this comparison is that an illustrated book like the *Comic History of England*, despite its blatantly satirical purpose, condenses a wealth of specifically historical material and serves as an index of the "reality effects" prized during the Romantic period. I began this chapter with Haskell's useful example of the seventeenth-century images of Pharamond, and it will be clear that, following my earlier analysis, the Joan of Moreau's engraving relates to the purely syntactic variations of the earlier period rather

3. The wooden William Wallace: John Leech, illustration to the *Comic History of England* (1851–52).

than to the acute specificity of Leech. This proposition enables us to frame a response to a further, related question that Haskell brings up in his skeptical review of the tide of historical images that sweeps through Britain and France in the early part of the nineteenth century. He singles out for comment Barante's *Histoire des Ducs de Bourgogne*, which in its successive editions did indeed accumulate numerous illustrations. Noting the fact that the 1842 edition contained numerous picturesque embellishments by Romantic artists whose conceits may appear fanciful to us today, he then asks; "What . . . did Prosper de Barante make of interpretations of this kind?" (Haskell, 298). The implication is that just as he was concerned in the preface to his history to vindicate the historian's claims over those of the historical novelist, so he would have been somewhat disconcerted by the arbitrary nature of visual recreations such as Achille Devéria's sentimental *Death of the Duchess of Orléans*. This may indeed have been so. But what is surely clear is that the historian who detected and wrote about the "historical fever" of his own times would not have been surprised at all by the fact that this expressed itself through a limitless thirst for the visual as well as the narrative representation of the past. Barante certainly understood that the good conscience of the professional historian could not ultimately act as a control on this social demand, even though it was his duty and opportunity to help to meet it. When, in the 1840s, he officially proposed the acceptance of the collection of Alexandre du Sommerard, housed in the Hôtel de Cluny, by the French state, he was unequivocal about the drawing power of the historical objects Du Sommerard had assembled, arguing, "The sword of a great warrior, the insignia of a celebrated sovereign, the jewels of a great or an unhappy queen, the books in which a writer has traced a few notes, are so many relics which people like to see and which make a different impression from the dead letter of the volume where we read their history."[7] Of course, Barante's strategy as a public-minded peer of the realm, as well as a celebrated historian, was to respond to the "historical fever" with good, solid information: even the Musée de Cluny, once it had been cut adrift by the death of its idiosyncratic founder and chief guide, was to be comprehensively reorganized so as to ensure that the search for knowledge, rather than mere curiosity, would be its governing theme. But the historian who was willing to recognize that history could remain a "dead letter" would surely not have been too disconcerted to witness his own historical work as it moved with the times, taking on a new visual dimension in proportion to the disposition of the Romantic audience to treat such representations as real.

If Barante himself was divided—like the other historians we have enumerated—in his recognition that "historical fever" produced effects that the professional historian could not hope to control, it is surely quite unnecessary for us to remain in thrall to the superegos of such long-departed pioneers. For those who wish to make sense of the phenomenon of historical-mindedness in the Romantic epoch, and its consequences for the contemporary world, the historian in the Rankean mold does not offer a solution; indeed he is part of the problem. The myth of "as it really happened" needs to be seen as part of the continuum of historical representation rather than as the endorsement of the professional historian's claim to dismiss all that occurs outside his field as cognitively inferior.

6

The Splitting of Historical Consciousness

If the model of the professional historian created in the early nineteenth century is, for the purposes of this study, part of the problem rather than the solution, it is nonetheless true that some of the major intellectual figures of the century provide invaluable instruments for decoding the significance of Romantic historical-mindedness. Behind Michel Foucault's *Archaeology of Knowledge* (1969), with its relentless drive to unmask the mythic underpinning of the cult of the past, lies the thought of Marx and Nietzsche. Marx's perceptive analysis of the role-playing element in historical representation has already been noted and will certainly come to mind again at later stages of my argument. Nietzsche's tripartite division of the relationship to the past has been evoked only briefly, but its exceptional value as a way of diagnosing the plurality of nineteenth-century historical attitudes, and their significance for representation, will be stressed in the latter part of this chapter.

The question arises as to whether the third of the great demythologizing thinkers of the previous century can contribute to our inquiry. Freud is, of course, for Foucault partly a historical symptom of the tendency of oppressive reason to impose its concepts upon the conditions of human existence that are least capable of exhibiting their own rationale: those of mental illness, criminality, and subversive sexuality. But it would be wrong to dismiss, in our particular investigation, the immense contribution Freud has made to the development of the concept of representation. In particular, it may be said that Freud and his followers have massively increased our ability to discern the meanings of the visual image, both as a symptom (here my own readings of images can be acknowledged to be, in the general sense, symptomatic) and as an integral element in the structure of representation that binds the individual subject to the social world. Having no place for the reductive interpretation sometimes practiced under the name of Freudianism, this study will still embody some crucial Freudian assumptions, one of which is that images have a privileged role in constructing individual and social identity: historical images are thus especially important in assessing how profoundly the rise of history in the nineteenth century marked the popular consciousness of the Western world.

Victor Burgin touches upon the issue of Freud's significance for the study of representation in a lucid essay published in his collection *The End of Art Theory* (1986). As he explains, "we become what we are only through our encounter, while growing up, with the multitude of representations of what we *may* become . . . There is no essential self which precedes the social *construction* of the self through the agency of representations." Thus, when the newly born child is the occasion of a question it does not yet understand—"Doctor, is it a boy or a girl?"—"the answer to that question will determine the general form of the demands society will make of us."[1] Burgin goes on to talk of the different stereotypes of male or female behavior that the child will encounter, and probably adopt, in the course of growing up. But, of course, images may be used—perhaps must be used—to complicate and in some ways subvert the stereotypes. As Marina Warner shows in the previously quoted article (and a series of other writings), personified images of the female body can be used, and most often are used, to entrench socially acceptable models of what it is to be a prospective wife and mother. But the image of Joan of Arc supplies a more complicated vehicle for identification: as a figure, derived from history, who combines "maidlike" qualities and the unlikely but historically attested attribute of martial valor, she can serve in the process of agitation for women's rights, as indeed in the war effort on behalf of a temporarily overrun French territory. Of course, the efficacy of Joan of Arc as such a symbol implied stretching the parameters of her historical personality to accord with the needs of the later period. But it may well be asked, where but in history can we find so rich a potential store of figures who would lend themselves not only to stereotyping but also to subverting the stereotype?

This is a perspective that can be only lightly sketched in at this point. It is necessary to evoke it, however, because it brings into focus one of the main mechanisms discussed by Freud, which has a special bearing on the issues of representation. In examining the way in which the self develops in early life, Freud found it necessary to dwell upon the "metamorphosis" of the child's relationship to his or her parents and its link to the achievement of a fully fledged superego. As Freud puts it: "The basis of the process is what is called 'identification'—that is to say, the assimilation of one ego to another one, as a result of which the first ego behaves like the second in certain respects, imitates it and in a sense takes it up into itself."[2] In working out this theory of identification, Freud concentrates initially on the male child's relationship to the biological father. But it is obvious that the concept can be applied, in a pertinent as well as a more diffuse way, to the individual subject's self-construction in and through the world of representation invoked by Burgin. Rarely are the vehicles for identification simple ones in the modern world; indeed Marina Warner carefully points out in her article on Joan of Arc how her use as a "womanly model" in American culture constituted "a vision of the French Middle Ages channelled through American male gallantry" (Warner, 108). Even such a compromised vision, however, counts as an indication of the role of history, and in particular the historical image, in establishing the common change of social and cultural awareness.

There is a further Freudian concept that should be mentioned here, since it is even more integrally connected to the sense of sight. This is the concept of fetishism. The fetish has, of course, a well-established significance in the domain of anthropology, where it is defined as an object that stands in for another one, concentrating upon itself a mystical or sexual power. Freud himself cites as an example from "social psychology" the way in which the Chinese mutilate the female foot, "then revering it like a fetish after it has been mutilated."[3] This example is used to establish the point that all such customs which locate a special power in a partial or delimited object are derived in the last analysis from a sexual scenario: "the fetish is a substitute for the woman's (the mother's) penis that the little boy once believed in and . . . does not want to give up" (Freud, 352). As Victor Burgin emphasizes, what Freud has done is to posit a "primary contributory cause" for a phenomenon that has been assumed to have special explanatory power within other social and political discourses: the obvious example is Marx's well-developed notion of "commodity fetishism" (Burgin, 43). He has also connected fetishism inseparably with the "scopic drive"—the desire to see. It would be puzzling indeed if the "desire for history" that we have formulated as a primary ground for the analysis of historical representation were to be entirely unconnected with this concept. "Desire for history" (Barante's "curiosity" or "historical fever") is after all inevitably involved in a dialectic of loss and recovery: the past is irretrievably past, and yet through the substitute object its pastness is somehow disavowed.

These Freudian concepts will be important, though hardly of prime significance, in several of the ensuing discussions. If they are not more to the fore, this is principally because of the exceptional pertinence of Nietzsche's ideas, in *The Use and Abuse of History*, which to a remarkable extent subsume the most important features of Freud's (and to some extent, Marx's) approach without being overly reductive. Nietzsche allows us to see how the phenomena he describes and discriminates could be described over again, with a more Marxist or Freudian slant. But his own text has the inestimable advantage of being situated right at the center of the issue of historical consciousness, which Nietzsche himself was perhaps the first to consider in so illuminating a way.

Deeply aware as he was of the momentous developments in historical culture that had spread throughout the Western world in the century following the French Revolution, Nietzsche was at the same time capable of formulating the needs of historical existence as giving rise to a number of possible choices: "history" is not treated as an absolute, as in the historicist orthodoxy, but as a spectrum of possible, lived relationships to the past, which must each be tested for their applicability to "life." Marx, it is true, began his *Eighteenth Brumaire* by acknowledging that "[t]he tradition of all the dead generations weighs like a nightmare on the brain of the living" (*EB*, 10). He then offers the encouraging prospect of how the revolutionary can transcend the "time-honored disguise" of history and learn to speak a new language. Nietzsche is not so optimistic. For him the "historical sense" is indeed capable of destroying living things, "be it a man or a people or a culture." But the solution to this problem can only lie in an appropriately fine calibration of the degree to which the past is allowed to bear down on us rather than in a Utopian annulment of history. "To fix this degree and the limits to the memory of the past . . . we must see clearly how great is the 'plastic power' of a man or a community or a culture" (*UAH*, 7).

The implications of this general attitude can be traced throughout this study, and Nietzsche's invocation of "plastic power" will resonate particularly towards the end. It is important to bear in mind, however, that Nietzsche's categories, in addition to providing a general critique, have an immediate operative value. Reference has been made already to his formulation of the "three ways" in which "history is necessary to the living man . . . These three relations answer to the three kinds of history—so far as they can be distinguished—the *monumental*, the *antiquarian*, and the *critical*" (*UAH*, 12). It remains for me to flesh out the substance of this distinction before showing its terms to be directly relevant to the analysis of a historical painting produced during the first flush of French Romanticism.

For Nietzsche, the "monumental" relation approximates quite closely to the categories we have already discussed in relation to Marx and Freud: it recalls Marx's vision of the French revolutionaries wearing Roman dress, as it does the Freudian concept of identification. Nietzsche, however, is more individualistic than Marx, and understandably more preoccupied than Freud with the historical (as opposed to the biological) dimension. He writes: "History is necessary above all to the man of action and power who fights a great fight and needs examples, teachers, and comforters; he cannot find them among his contemporaries" (*UAH*, 12). Nietzsche achieves a rare degree of eloquence in conjuring up this image of the past as a dimension in which the lonely modern can take comfort, drawing from "the knowledge that the great thing existed and was therefore possible, and so may be possible again." Such a realization will be aided by the discovery that the great figures of the past themselves developed a "monumental" relationship to their predecessors in an earlier, "classic" age. Thus, the contemporary German educational reformers of Nietzsche's own times "will gather strength from the remembrance that the culture of the Renaissance was raised on the shoulders of such another band of a hundred men" (*UAH*, 14).

Yet the subtlety of Nietzsche's approach is conveyed in the fact that each distinctive relation to the past implies a particular drawback as well as a specific advantage. The problem with monumentalism is that it presupposes a view of history in which the cycles of history continually repeat themselves (the Stoic view that St. Augustine so roundly condemned in the *City of God*). As Nietzsche himself writes: "Only if the earth always began its drama again after the fifth act, and it was certain that the same interaction of motives, the same *deus ex machina*, the same catastrophe would recur at particular intervals, could the man of action venture to look for the whole archetypic truth in monumental history" (*UAH*, 15).

Nietzsche is well aware that the "monumental" approach embodies a very traditional attitude to history, perhaps the most traditional of all, and it is not always easy to distinguish between a "monumental" past and a "mythical romance" that bears no relation to history. But the "antiquarian" approach, which he then goes on to contrast with the monumental, is a more modern strategy: indeed Nietzsche is in particular noteworthy for the way in which he expatiates eloquently on a disposition of mind that had been cultivated especially in the preceding century, and in his own native Germany. According to this disposition of mind, "history is necessary to the man of conservative and reverent nature who looks back to the origins of his existence with love and trust" (*UAH*, 17). Scarcely has Nietzsche begun to sketch out this antiquarian personality, so different from that of the "man of action," when he is drawn irresistibly to the concrete specification of objects: "The possession of his ancestors' furniture changes its meaning in his soul, for his soul is rather possessed by it. All that is small and limited, moldy and obsolete, gains a worth and inviolability of its own from the conservative and reverent soul of the antiquary migrating into it and building a secret nest there. The history of his town becomes the history of himself" (*UAH*, 18).

For the antiquarian, then, the relation to the past is established not through "example" but through furniture: through the introjection (as the psychoanalyst might say) of the "good object" handed down from the past. Does this concern to lend "worth and inviolability" to objects of no intrinsic value run the danger of fetishism? Obviously, in the way that Nietzsche states the matter here, it does. And we can quite easily appreciate that he will find substantial arguments against the antiquarian approach when its "very limited field" and its tendency to turn away from the life of the present day are taken into account. But the really interesting point is that Nietzsche has found room for the description of an attitude which, by the latter part of the nineteenth century, was habitually regarded as the unavowable, disreputable side of historical consciousness.

He selects inspiring examples to illustrate the antiquarian approach, such as Goethe before Strasbourg Cathedral, the "monument of Erwin von Steinbach": "the storm of his feeling rent the historical cloud-veil that hung between them." He is even able to cite the case of a great contemporary German historian, whose antiquarian zeal rises to the point where all objects are renounced in favor of an ideal (but diffused) aura of historicity: "Niebuhr confesses that he could live happily on a moor among free peasants with a history and would never feel the want of art" (*UAH*, 18).

Nietzsche's categories have not yet attained the sophistication of Riegl, who (in the previously cited essay) discriminates "age-value" from "historical value," and both from any form of "art-value" (see Riegl 1982, 31–38). But he is at the same time astonishingly open in his recognition of the multiple types of modern investment in the historical past. In each of the previous categories, he is discussing the relation to history not as a mere luxury, or a domain of self-delusion, but as a necessity, first and foremost. This does not, however, stop him from acknowledging in the last resort that the "critical" attitude is also necessary and that its essential component is the will to deal roughly with—even to reject completely—the legacy of the past. As Nietzsche expresses it: "Man must have the strength to break up the past, and apply it, too, in order to live. He must bring the past to the bar of judgment, interrogate it remorselessly, and finally condemn it. Every past is worth condemning" (*UAH*, 20–21).

Hayden White draws attention in *Metahistory* to the way in which historians like Tocqueville, and Nietzsche's friend Burckhardt, used the trope of irony, or what Vico had called "double vision." To a great extent, as we follow Nietzsche's careful exposition of the contrasted attitudes of the "monumental" and the "antiquarian," we feel that we are being exposed to an ironic perspective: neither of the two views can be privileged, and neither cancels the other out. But the critical perspective goes further than irony: it is a conclusive distancing of the self from the examples, as well as the comforts, of history; it is a negation of the past and, in the same measure, an affirmation of what Nietzsche considered to be the overriding interest of "life." Nevertheless, the conclusion of the discussion reinstates, as least provisionally, a certain notion of equilibrium: "Every man and nation needs a certain knowledge of the past, whether it be through monumental, antiquarian, or critical history, according to his objects, powers, and necessities" (*UAH*, 22).

It is scarcely necessary to point out that Nietzsche's achievement consists in the power of his written exhortation rather than in any practical exposition of the way in which nations and individuals could perform the perilous balancing act of reconciling the monumental, the antiquarian, and the critical. But this is not to say that his tripartite analysis of the "necessity" of history is without consequences for the assessment and discrimination of different forms of historical-mindedness from the Romantic period to the present day. One might say that historical understanding had, up to that point, been impeded by the almost uncontested observation that there was a good and a bad side to the study of the past: as with the professional historians who struggled to neutralize, and appropriate for themselves, the colorful creatures of the historical novelist, it was a question of justifying the attraction to past times by vaunting the stern, scientific claims of the new professional historiography. Nietzsche, however, shows us—at least as a Utopian prospect— the possibility of accommodating and reconciling different relations to history within a single, harmonious spectrum.

Yet Nietzsche's distinctions are also useful for analyzing the ways in which the representation of history exposed the fault lines existing between the different relations to the past. They help us to discern the uneasy coexistence of "monumental" and "antiquarian" attitudes and the role these attitudes perform in the development and succession of representational forms. Once again, a visual example has been selected to demonstrate in a vivid manner the way in which historical materials are being worked through at an important juncture in the early history of Romantic painting. At the same time, the painting about to be discussed evokes the intense patterns of ideological conflict that were being generated in the period following the fall of the Napoleonic Empire.

As was noted at the outset of this study, the French nation experienced with a particular acuity the turbulent history of the years following the Revolution. For the French, the notion of the "ancien régime" was invested with particularly ambivalent feelings, since it figured at the same time as an oppressive system from which the efforts of the revolutionaries had emancipated the nation and as the mysterious realm of "la vieille France"—now lost forever, and for that reason irresistibly attractive to the imagination. Napoleon's determination to inaugurate a new style of government was never more than partially successful, and it might be argued that the very relentlessness of his desire to make a clean break with the past—

the design of new uniforms for himself and his court, the borrowing of Egyptian mannerisms to create an "Empire" style—helped to stimulate a nostalgic reversion to the national past. Prosper de Barante, as an imperial "sous-préfet" advancing in his career, spent his leisure time editing the memoirs of a heroine of the Vendée wars, Mme de La Rochejaquelein. Having experienced firsthand the gigantic reach of the new Empire, he preferred to study the local characteristics of the region of northwestern France, which had thrown in its lot with the Bourbon monarchy and suffered a bloody repression as a result.

The fall of Napoleon, and the restoration of the Bourbon dynasty in the person of Louis XVIII, thus posed a particularly acute problem, and offered a corresponding opportunity, for those engaged in the representation of the past. How would it be possible to tap the legacy of "la vieille France"? How could the visual artists, in particular, provide icons establishing the continuity of French history, while simultaneously acknowledging their debt to David and the painters of the revolutionary school?

◆

In the French salon of 1819, Marie-Philippe Coupin de la Couperie (1773–1851) exhibited, to great acclaim, his large historical painting: *Sully Showing His Grandson the Monument Containing the Heart of Henri IV at La Flèche*. In 1820 it entered the collection of the Duchesse de Berry, wife of the heir to the newly restored Bourbon throne, and has ended up as part of the large collection of works of art (many of them dating from the Restoration) in the National Museum of the Château de Pau, Henri IV's birthplace. No special imagination is needed to conceive why the cult of Henri IV became a notable feature of the visual arts in the period following Napoleon's downfall. Henri IV was the founder of the Bourbon dynasty and, moreover, a king specially associated with the reconciliation of warring factions in the interests of national unity. The fat and gouty Louis XVIII could profit from any invocation of this unimpeachable national figure. The question remained, however: how was this hero to be represented?

Coupin de la Couperie decided on a strategy that does not lack originality. Henri IV was assassinated by the Jesuit Ravaillac in 1610, and after his death "his body was carried with great ceremony to St. Denis, where he was buried, and his heart to La Flèche to the College of the Jesuits, which he had founded, and where we see a marble tomb to the left-hand side of the high altar in the crossing of the church."[4] So runs the account in Anselme's *Histoire de la Maison Royale de France*, compiled in the eighteenth century. In fact, by the Restoration period (and following the expulsion of the Jesuits from France), the erstwhile College of the Jesuits had been turned into a well-known military academy, where Coupin de la Couperie served briefly as drawing master in 1815. It is easy to imagine that this former soldier in the imperial armies, nominated to La Flèche in the year of Waterloo, would have been struck by the conjuncture between the new military academy, whose vocation was to serve the constitutional monarchs of Restoration France, and the prestigious symbol of the former glories of the House of Bourbon, now acquiring a new contemporaneity and significance.

Coupin de la Couperie therefore paints the former Jesuit church, the Eglise St. Louis. He paints it as architecture, in a meticulous, somewhat dry style, recording the fine detail of the stonework of the monument and a large section of the adjacent high altar as well. All that we see of Henri IV is the gilded inscription (no doubt much deteriorated by the Restoration period) and the gold and glowing sculptured heart, attended by allegorical figures who indeed seem to start from their niches to celebrate his virtue and his fame. There is, in fact, also a head and shoulder bust of the departed king installed in a roundel at the summit of the composition, but this is gray and unexciting. The focus of our attention is undoubtedly the plump golden heart, cushioned with laurel wreaths and sur-mounted by a crown, to which our eyes travel after they have read the inscription.

But it is not the spectator, outside the picture, who is envisaged as the primary scrutineer of this scene. Coupin can legitimately show the marble tomb as being in tip-top condition because his title denotes an event taking place hardly more than twenty years after the assassination of Henri IV—an event that is certainly not com-memorated as being historically significant but that no doubt formed part of the folklore of La Flèche. Let us assume that the date is 1630. Henri IV's faithful counselor, the Duc de Sully, would then have been over seventy and out of power for many years. His grandson, Maximilien-François, Prince de Henrichemont and future second Duc de Sully, would have been sixteen years of age. No special act of imagination is needed to conceive that this visit might have taken place, since Sully habitually resided in his Château de Villebon, near Chartres, in his later years and was himself buried at Nogent-

4. The monumental infiltrated by the antiquarian: Coupin de la Couperie, *Sully Showing His Grandson the Monument Containing the Heart of Henri IV at La Flèche* (1819).

le-Rotrou, a further property on the route to La Flèche. It has even been suggested that he chose this place for his tomb because the cortege bearing the heart of Henri IV rested there on its journey to La Flèche.[5]

Coupin therefore paints Sully as the faithful servant of the great king, displaying the monument to the grandson who carries his own hopes for the future (Sully's son, in effect, quarreled with him and ultimately predeceased him). What could be clearer as a demonstration of the *monumental* relation to the past, as Coupin reinterprets the affecting story to suit a new generation—those military cadets with whom he was briefly in contact at La Flèche and later, on a more long-term basis, at the academy of St.-Cyr? Surely the two levels of interpretation dovetail impeccably? On the one hand, we have the minister and disciple who exhibits the monument of his master as an exemplum to the young: Sully was, in fact, dedicated to the idea of history as example in the most literal way, compiling a verse set of *Parallèles de César et de Henri le Grand* in the tradition of Plutarch, which he published in 1615.[6] On the other hand, we have the nineteenth-century historical painter, whose idea it is to create a stirring image for the Restoration period, rooted in his own experience as a teacher of the French soldiers of the future.

The reason why this is not an adequate interpretation of Coupin's work is precisely because it neglects, or at least takes for granted, the mechanisms the artist has used, irrespective of their effects in and through representation. Coupin was working within a specific tradition: as a pupil and friend of Anne-Louis Girodet, he was well acquainted with one of the great and original artists of the imperial epoch, himself a pupil of Jacques-Louis David. Thus, it is worth asking straightaway a more complex question than has been prompted by any of the foregoing discussions: in what way does this "exemplary," or "monumental," theme imply Coupin's modification or transformation of the existing conventions of historical painting current in France? Here there is a useful clue to Coupin's practice in what may be considered a significant, if surprising, source for the figure of the aged Sully, lost in thought. The fine profile and the white ruff are certainly not inconsistent with the image of the statesman that we find on his splendid tomb at Nogent-le-Rotrou. This, however, displays him as being altogether more alert and forceful. For the bowed head and grizzled locks even in profile, not to mention the posture of the seated body seen from

5. The grieving Plato as a neoclassical forerunner to Sully: David, *Death of Socrates* (1787).

the side, we can surely evoke one of the most striking and famous of David's exemplary paintings: *Death of Socrates* (1787). Sully's figure, as shown by Coupin, closely resembles the grieving figure of Plato who was added to the group of Socrates' disciples despite historical testimony that he was not present on the fateful occasion.

Where does this leave us? I suggest that it shows how Coupin's picture, conceived as an exemplary one, is in fact fundamentally inconsistent in its effects. But, at the same time, this inconsistency can be regarded precisely as the index of a greater historicity, which was already working through and was shortly to transform the language of pictorial representation. It would be wrong to oversimplify the message of David's *Socrates*, which is itself (as Norman Bryson has argued) a work giving rise to many possible ambiguities.[7] Nonetheless, for our purposes, it can be taken as demonstrating the intention to achieve a "monumental" relation to the past, in Nietzsche's sense. Francis Haskell has discussed under the category "Art as Prophecy" what he calls "the ruthlessly austere style that David (and a few others) had adopted for depicting public scenes of ancient virtue—at a time when public scenes of modern virtue seemed non-existent" (Haskell, 398). Retrospectively, at any rate, a major work like *Socrates* (which Napoleon himself vainly attempted to buy from its private owners) must have seemed to a painter like Coupin the optimal demonstration of how to use history for an exemplary purpose. Hence, perhaps, the "ruthlessly austere" way in which he, too, constructs the architectural decor in which the aged Sully passes on the lesson of history to a representative of modern youth, just as Socrates marks his passing in front of a well-composed frieze of young and old disciples, with the youth who hands him the hemlock catching our attention with the most emphatically displayed grief of all.

Yet, of course, the visual dynamics of Coupin's painting do not work in the same way as those of David's *Socrates*, and any comparison that starts from the basis of the similarity of the figures of Sully and Plato must immediately take this difference into account. David's work is horizontally organized, with a friezelike structure that allows the diversity of Socrates' followers to be fully expressed, though a deep space opens up beyond Plato's head to show Xanthippe (Socrates' wife) being escorted out of the prison. Coupin's work follows the soaring architecture of the Eglise St. Louis, allowing our gaze to travel up, by way of the young spectator, to the glowing heart at the apex of the composition. By showing us the youth's back, however, it effects a curious displacement of psychological interest. Since no expression is visible, we linger on the purely decorative detail of the carefully assembled seventeenth-century dress: from the smart boots, with their shining spurs, across the casually draped velvet cloak and the golden sash, to the luxuriant ringlets of the young prince's coiffure. The picturesque assembly of flags, caught in the light by the transept window, echoes this deliberate emphasis on the surface of things, as if the cold stone backdrop were being used simply to set off the quicksilver vitality of this vision of youth in awe of age. The old Sully's face is the only place where we can read anything more specific, and, though it borrows the gravity of David's Plato, it simultaneously strives for a sentimental rather than a stoic note: from the corner of the old man's eye, there squeezes a large and luminous tear.

Coupin's painting is of special interest as an essay in historical representation, since it was conceived as a "monumental" statement (in Nietzsche's sense) but has resulted in something more closely akin to the "antiquarian." It attempts a new version of the exemplary Neoclassical work—one suitable to the changed political circumstances of the Bourbon Restoration—but in moving from the ideal generality of the classical exemplum to the picturesque specificity of the age of Henri IV, it subverts its own didactic purpose. Instead of underlining Henri IV's claim to be a great national hero, comparable with Caesar in Sully's own estimation, it intimates (even if it does not fully accept) that the pleasure of the period decor must be its own reward. So preoccupied is Coupin with giving visual interest to displaced and incidental detail—the golden heart rather than the bust, the spur, the ringlets and the gilt trimmings of the seventeenth-century costume—that he invests the whole image with what the Freudian would see as a fetishistic character—though the antiquarian, in Nietzsche's terms, might claim that to be a legitimate component of an intense relation to the objects of the past.

At a later stage, I shall be looking at several additional aspects of this productive crisis in historical representation, which is especially strong in Restoration France. In particular, the implications of the Bourbon cult of Henri IV will be seen to have produced fascinating transformations and revisions, in the quest for an authenticity that was itself closely bound up with contemporary political interests. For the present, it is worth making just one further comparison to add to the series of David and Coupin. Richard Parkes Bonington's *A Knight and Page* (c. 1826), in the Yale Center for British Art, is a painting of specially illustrious provenance, having been given by the English artist to his friend, Eugène Delacroix. It is an oil painting, possibly unfinished, which appears to have been the product of some careful and imaginative historical research: Bonington probably derived the features of the "knight" from his study of the bronze of the *condottiere* Bartolemmeo Colleoni, by Verrocchio, which he saw in Venice, and it is likely that he intended the austere figure to represent the hero of Goethe's historical drama, Goetz von Berlichingen.[8] Whether or not this identification holds (and the very uncertainty is, in a sense, a measure of Bonington's artistic success), the *Knight and Page* is a brilliant feat of historical staging. Dramatizing as it does the relationship of youth and maturity—the young page and the heroic knight—it nevertheless does so within a scene whose psychological aspects are as deliberately unclear as its spatial aspects are ambiguous. The page has one foot on the level where the knight stands, but the knight seems to have his attention fixed by an event on another plane—something that is taking place beyond the decorated surface of the hanging that sets off the page's head. There is a strong sense of what, in the theater, would be described as "off-stage," but this paradoxically increases the suggestiveness of the represented scene by annexing it to something we can only conceive in our imagination. Here, indeed, in the sphere of pictorial representation, is what Barthes calls the "reality effect."

Bonington's painting, like David's, is secure within its own convention of representation. But Delacroix was right to stress the important role played in his technique by the use of color: it is indeed the color values of the *Knight and Page* (the broad alternation of passages of scarlet and gold against the black backdrop) that found the composition and establish it as a unified field. In this context, Coupin's work can be seen as a not altogether satisfactory halfway house between the dry equality of plastic treatment favored by David and the broad color and nervous touch associated with Bonington. In that transition, from the ancien régime to the Restoration, and from neoclassicism to Romanticism in painting, the possibility opens up for a more concrete and more imaginative use of historical representation that will develop and manipulate effects congenial to the new historical-mindedness of the nineteenth century. Coupin, a painter of the intermediate generation, does not achieve this; his work is, however, interesting precisely because of the way in which it testifies to his ambivalent relationship to the representation of the past. The "splitting" of historical consciousness, which was later theorized by Nietzsche, finds in this painting an appropriate, if disconcerting, form.

Part 3

History as Discourse

7

Taking a Subjective Stance

What does it mean to assume a subjective relationship to the past? Essentially, it is the argument of this study that such a question acquires significance in the context of the newly developed historical-mindedness of the Romantic epoch. Through tracking a series of individual antiquarians, collectors, and men of letters over the period from the latter part of the eighteenth century to the end of the nineteenth century, we can appreciate the escalating stakes attached to historical subjectivity and the astonishing variety of forms in which the relationship was made manifest. But there is a second question that follows directly upon the first. How is the subjective relationship, and the formal expression that is its consequence, to be analyzed? Much of the work done on historical representation in this period has been purely descriptive and accumulative, as if the writer were a bemused anthropologist trying to record the curious practices of a remote society; or, alternatively, it has held fast to the cognitive criteria of the professional historian and perpetuated the uneasy quarantine that Ranke's generation tried to maintain against the incursions of the fictional past.

By contrast, my own approach (following Hayden White and Roland Barthes, as well as nineteenth-century figures like Nietzsche) has been to open up the field of representation to structural and rhetorical analysis, showing how the visual image, whose indeterminate relation to the documentary evidence of written sources has been a frequent cause of uncertainty, condenses precious data about the state of historical awareness. The next stage in my argument is to emphasize the special role of subjectivity in the whole process of historical representation. As I mentioned before, Barthes is the first analyst to draw attention to the fact that history is both *histoire* and *discours*. In terms of Benveniste's important distinction, it can be seen without difficulty that it is *histoire*, indeed the definitive form of *histoire*. Benveniste defines an ideal at least for a nineteenth-century historian like Ranke or Barante when he explains, "It is a question of the presentation of the facts that took place at a certain moment of time, without any intervention of the speaker in the account *(récit)*" (Benveniste, 239). But Barthes rightly points out that in epochs preceding the nineteenth century, even the historian had thought it fit to intervene in his account, to acknowledge the help of a patron, to invoke the blessing of God, or simply to credit his sources. In this recognition, he recalls Benveniste's point that even in *histoire* we can pass "instantaneously" from one register to another: "Each time there appears within a historical account a discourse, when the historian for example reproduces the words of a personage or intervenes himself to judge the events recounted, we pass to another temporal system, that of discourse" (Benveniste, 242).

My strategy is to expand the category of history as discourse far beyond what Barthes thought appropriate in his essay, concerned as he was with the nineteenth-century historian's attempt to achieve a mythic self-immolation before the real. Discourse, in my analysis, is established when a form of utterance or speech (in the widest sense) bears the marks of the speaker's agency; instead of effacing these marks and insisting on the "pastness" of the past, the speaker manifestly assumes the role of the author of the discourse. Clearly, this means that a given set of historical data can change from the historical to the discursive articulation, in accordance with the presence or absence of such a speaker. For instance, a collection (like that of Alexandre du Sommerard) is discursive insofar as the collector assumes a public role, as guide and commentator guaranteeing the historicity and status of the individual objects. When it becomes a museum (like the Musée de Cluny in the 1840s), it inevitably loses this discursive character to a greater or lesser degree, and the order of the collection is assumed to have its own intrinsic, given quality, its own "pastness."

Yet the example of the fully fledged historical museum comes at a fairly advanced stage in the process I shall be describing. The question that needs to be asked, first of all, is, when and how did "subjects" (poets, artists, historians) begin to intervene discursively in the story of the past? This is an issue that leads us back to the very beginning of the Romantic epoch, indeed to the period often termed "preromantic," when the major transformations of thought and sensibility were still, as it were, in embryo.

Johann Winckelmann is often held to be the father of art criticism, as well as the father of art history. The fact that he is equally important as a figure in the genealogy of these two areas of practice that have increasingly drifted apart discloses a factor of some interest. For this German writer who resided in Rome and studied the antiquities of Italy (though not those of Greece) firsthand was notable for his capacity to evoke in splendidly charged poetic language the subject matter and style of classical sculpture; he created a language of intense and vivid response to the art object, which was at the same time a mode of inserting it in narrative—of setting it within the contours of a mythic story line. But Winckelmann was nonetheless concerned, as few admirers of ancient art had been before him, with setting defensible historical boundaries within the artistic development of the Greeks and Romans. In his *History of Ancient Art* (1764), he responds in an extraordinarily empathetic way to individual works, without for a moment losing sight of the need for a clear historical perspective. Thus in his famous passage on the mutilated *Torso Belvedere*, he evokes the mythic context ("in that powerfully developed chest we behold in imagination the breast against which the giant Geryon was squeezed"), but returns in the end to a sober historical estimate: "The *Torso* appears to be one of the last perfect works which art produced in Greece before the loss of its freedom."[1]

Winckelmann's impassioned evocations of classical Greek sculpture mark the emergence of a discourse of art criticism, in which the critic asserts a subjective role as empathetic commentator on the work. Yet this is not in the strict sense a historical commentary, however careful Winckelmann may be to attribute the various works to their respective periods. As the passage on the *Torso Belvedere* makes clear, the time he conjures up imaginatively is a mythic time, one appropriate to the exploits of the demigod Hercules, and not the historical time of the sculpture's fabrication. For the empathetic imagination and the historical sense to combine, no doubt, it was necessary for the writer's attention to be grasped by a period that did not present, as a substitute for historical knowledge, the dazzling apparatus of myth. It was necessary for the historical sense and the mythic imagination to work hand in hand, which meant, in effect, the opening up of a historical domain so little known that it still had to be enlivened by vivid and compelling narratives.

This is what turned out to be the case when another, even more celebrated German writer encountered a historical object of grandiose proportions. The writer was Goethe and the object Strasbourg Cathedral, which he got to know in successive visits during the early 1770s. In his *Autobiography*, Goethe makes it clear that initially he was hardly prepared to observe dispassionately, let alone to take a lively interest in, the venerable building. He writes: "what I could not quite clearly make out, the first or following time, was that I regarded this miracle as something monstrous, which must have terrified me, if it had not at the same time appeared to me comprehensible by its regularity."[2] Goethe conveys in an extremely direct way the struggle of a person who has been taught to consider the classical aesthetic property of "regularity" as the mark of good art and architecture but who recognizes that the strong impression he has received from this outlandish work cannot altogether be explained away in these terms. One possible strategy of coping with the discordance is to invoke the newly popularized aesthetic of the "sublime" and to suggest that the "unity" of the cathedral lies at a higher level of synthesis:

> The more I considered the facade . . . the more was that first impression strengthened and developed that here the sublime has entered into alliance with the pleasing. If the vast, when it comes before us as a mass, is not to terrify, if it is not to confuse when we try to investigate its details, it must enter into an unnatural, apparently impossible connection, it must associate itself with the pleasing. But, since now, it will only be possible for us to speak of the impression of the cathedral, if we think of those two irreconcilable qualities as united, so we already see from this in what high value we must hold this ancient monument. (Goethe, 334)

Both this passage, and the long subsequent discussion of the architectural features of the cathedral, make it clear that Goethe was struggling with the primary question: how do we *see* this building? He had not reached the stage of being able to ask: how do we *read* this cathedral? A century later, a critic like Ruskin could, in his aptly named *Bible of Amiens*, range all over the massive structure of such a building, picking up the details of its mass of sculptural embellishment and treating them as the open book of medieval life. But Goethe was still transfixed by the problem of how so aesthetically excessive a structure could be accommodated within the canons of eighteenth-century taste. The solution he found—even if he repudiated its implications in later years—was to be a dramatic and unexpected one, which had the advantage of eclipsing, for a time at least, the inconvenient mass of the structure itself. In his work *On German Architecture*, published at the end of 1772 after his first visits to the cathedral but omitted from his collected works, he conceived of a brilliant device for dramatizing and humanizing his relationship to the problematic building: his text was to be a panegyric to the architect of Strasbourg Cathedral, Erwin von Steinbach, whose memorial stone he had been unable to discover, despite diligent inquiry. It was to be a recognition of the fact that in the cathedral Erwin had built his own monument, and so created the emblem of a specifically German form of architecture. More so than in the *Autobiography*, Goethe acknowledges the specifically nationalistic aspect of his conversion to the "Gothic" taste:

> When I first went to the cathedral, my head was filled with general notions of taste. I honored by hearsay the principles of the harmony of masses and purity of forms, and was the declared enemy of the confused capriciousness of Gothic ornament. Under the heading of Gothic, as in a dictionary article, I had compiled all the synonymous misunderstandings concerning the ill-defined, the disordered, unnatural, pieced-together, patched-up, and overladen which had ever passed through my mind. No wiser than a people which calls "barbaric" all the world it does not know, I called *gothic* whatever did not fit my system. I made no distinction between the contorted, painted puppets and decorations with which our noble bourgeois fancify their houses and the awesome relics of our older German architecture.[3]

As will be clear from this passage, the young Goethe views his initial discomfiture before the Gothic cathedral not only as an aesthetic mistake but as a failure in national self-consciousness. Through the device of addressing his confessions to the German

master architect, he simultaneously explores the structure of the
originally inaccessible building and defines his own position with
respect to the growing sense of German national identity. *Of German
Architecture* marks his turning "towards my fatherland, towards my
love." But in his *Third Pilgrimage to Erwin's Grave* (1776), he goes so
far as to picture himself ascending "from one level to the next of
the great structure, meditating on the identity of the creative power
in the artist and the creative power in Nature" (as the recent biography by Nicholas Boyle puts it); he is finally at the very top of the
cathedral tower when his companion, tired of waiting, joins him
and interrupts "the moment of 'devotion.'"[4] This is the moment
where the fragmentary text breaks off, and Boyle is surely right
to stress its exceptional value in demonstrating the link between
Goethe's symbolic life, of which this "pilgrimage" is such a notable
feature, and his future development as a writer.

Strasbourg Cathedral was at this point in history (and had been
for some time) on French soil. Yet this in no way interferes with the
significance of Goethe's literary encounter with the great medieval
building or obscures the place it came to occupy in his development
as both a writer and a German patriot. Through his friendship with
the philosopher Johann Herder, Goethe was already, by the early
1770s, well acquainted with the widespread revival of interest in
the medieval origins of German culture. His preoccupation with
the mythical figure of Erwin von Steinbach, whose memory was
far from fresh in the city of Strasbourg, coincided with his preparatory work on the drama *Goetz von Berlichingen*, whose even more
mythical hero was the free imperial knight of that name, later to
inspire Bonington (see Boyle, 116–17). In opening up this area of
subject matter so foreign to the neoclassicism of his earlier work,
Goethe did not simply effect a transformation in style. He succeeded
in empowering his own historical imagination and enlarging that
of his contemporaries.

Yet this process took place (as we must keep in mind) against a
cultural backdrop that had hardly yet begun to change. For Goethe
to be so galvanized by the spectacle of a particular Gothic cathedral,
it was necessary for him to be invested with an almost unique blend
of discordant feelings and preconceptions: he had to be sufficiently
permeated with the principles of "regularity" to regard Strasbourg
as "monstrous," sufficiently imaginative to recognize it nonetheless
as a "miracle," and sufficiently conversant with the movement of
German cultural revival to work out these contradictory impulses

for himself. The general awareness of such monuments was less discordant, and certainly more prosaic. René Lanson has asserted (though without further evidence) that the medieval cathedrals never lost their hold on the imaginations of the people, even in the century that stressed most vigorously the need for a simplified and decorous canon of forms. He writes: "The castles appeared monstrous to them, right up to the end of the [eighteenth] century when they discovered the Romantic aspect of their silhouette and the majesty of their mass; but the people always loved its cathedrals" (Lanson, 32). Despite this assurance, it is obvious that Goethe's subjective investment in the past produced a new way of valuing the Gothic monument, which was not simply the result of time-honored popular beliefs and practices.

Indeed, it is fair to say that Goethe's revaluation implied, to a certain extent, a decision to set aside the actual appearance of the cathedral as it was in the early 1770s and to substitute a perfect original, the seamless product of the art of Erwin von Steinbach. Winckelmann was confronted with sculptures that, like the *Torso Belvedere*, had been truncated over the years, and he responded with all the more eloquence to the task of restoring their mythic identity. Goethe was faced with a cathedral that, though not actually a ruin, was in the process of being repaired after a disastrous fire in 1759. The entire vault of the Gothic structure had been destroyed on this occasion, together with the octagonal lantern that dominated the choir. Prominent national architects had been consulted about the necessary repairs to the structure, and it was eventually decided to put up a new vault in wood, with a copper covering, and to replace the lantern with a new structure that would eventually form the base of a Gothic spire. The inhabitants of Strasbourg thus showed themselves to be attentive to the style and character of their most notable monument. But this did not prevent them from authorizing the construction of a series of "boutiques" (small shops and/or workshops) on the north and south sides of the cathedral. These pseudo-Gothic structures, designed by an architect named Goetz, were put up between 1772 and 1778, hence coinciding with at least the last stages of Goethe's re-creative engagement with the masterpiece of Erwin von Steinbach.

An engraving of the cathedral, dating from the last years of the eighteenth century, shows the great tower into which Goethe ascended; it also shows the boutiques clustered at the base of the flying buttresses and the new octagonal structure that has by this

6. Goethe's Strasbourg Cathedral, with added contemporary
boutiques and a telegraphic signaling device topping the Octagon:
engraving from the late eighteenth century.

time sprouted not a Gothic spire but a semaphore signaling device. The new invention of the Abbé Chappe, destined to improve national communications immeasurably from the time of the revolutionary wars onwards, is here proudly displayed on what was no doubt the most suitable structure for its operations. It is a powerful reminder of the fact that in eighteenth-century France the "Gothic" was not simply a taste to be reviled and later rediscovered. The medieval cathedral might, from the point of view of the *philosophe*, stand for all that was benighted and superstitious about the remote Middle Ages. But it was also a physical fact, and as such it had to develop in accord with the requirements of its users, who had to react to the wear and tear of the ages or the sudden emergency of fire and flood in the most effective ways they could devise. As Lanson has pointed out, the massive reconstruction of the Cathedral of Orléans continued over virtually the whole of the eighteenth century, and on the whole the citizens resisted the notion of classicizing the structure in favor of a "Gothic" alternative, even though the architects of the period did not find it easy to emulate medieval building techniques (Lanson, 36–38).

So Strasbourg Cathedral was very far from being an object outside time, or an object that could be assessed as a wholly authentic product of the Middle Ages. It had come a long way since the times of Erwin von Steinbach. But, of course, to impose this criterion on eighteenth-century perceptions is itself anachronistic. Goethe was naturally more moved by the absence of a memorial to Erwin von Steinbach (an absence which he, in his own writing, could hope to make up for) than by the inconvenient presence of a new vault and a substitute for the original lantern. Only if he had himself had a firm and unequivocal idea of what constituted an authentic Gothic building would he have been struck by the anomaly of such modern contemporary additions. Only if he had been able to conceive of the specifically modern, or at least Postromantic notion of "restoration," would he have been capable of judging the physical appearance of the building in such terms.

The point can be made very simply. Goethe is not, like Winckelmann, concerned with pumping life into a stone fragment so that it will achieve a mythic identity independent of its historical status. In returning repeatedly to the masterpiece of Erwin von Steinbach, he is at the same time progressively discovering how "our older German architecture" can serve as a vital link to the pre-Modern period and as a means of reinforcing the new German sense of national identity. The subjective investment, however, in Goethe as in Winckelmann, necessarily sets up the object in a form of ideal existence: it is a discursive fact, produced by the cunning strategies of Goethe's verbal art, and not a cathedral that comes into view, and this cathedral, perhaps accessible to Goethe's readers, would not have been the building that confronted the inhabitants of Strasbourg in their everyday business. Already implicit in Goethe's powerful creation is the diagnosis made by the Romantic poet Victor Hugo of the long-term transition from a culture in which messages are transmitted by the emblematic facades of public monuments to one where the individual creator takes it upon him- or herself to re-create such public values through the medium of the written text. As Hugo predicts: "Le livre tuera l'édifice" (The book will kill the building).[5]

This does not, of course, imply that Goethe's vision must be seen in some sense as escapist, as a flight from reality into an imagined historical realm. For it is precisely the achievement of the Romantics, and their significant predecessors, to have created new, imaginatively accessible symbols through which the concrete experience of history could be interpreted and revised. Even if Goethe could have had no inkling of the complex judgments that would later be brought to bear on questions of authenticity and restoration, it is through texts like his that the Romantic generation learned to value, and indeed love, the past. The later sophistication of historical-mindedness depends, we might say, on the establishment of a primary relation of this kind.

Goethe's ability to focus on Strasbourg Cathedral as a potent reminder of "our older German architecture," and hence as a gauge of German identity, depended no doubt on the fact that Strasbourg was not at that time a German city. The fact that Alsace was a possession of the French crown supplied the original distance, or "otherness," on the basis of which Goethe was able to assert his subjective identification. This is a familiar point to be made when tracing the intricate patterns of subjective identification with the past. It is as if the historical object had to be brought into view, after initially being occluded, before its true significance could be appreciated. Goethe's success in investing a whole monument with this feature of renewed visibility was a virtually unique achievement, however. More often his European contemporaries, or those of them who shared his desire to open up the past, secured their relationship to the historical object through a more humdrum means of recognition. What was offered to view was what had been brought to the surface, after remaining for many centuries under the ground. The antiquarian sensibility depended, in an essential way, on the practice of archaeology.

In making this point, I do however run the risk of diluting the concept of historical identification—so powerful in Goethe's case—and associating it with the rather diffuse notions of antiquarianism and archaeology, as they were practiced in Europe, at least from the time of the Renaissance onwards. Francis Haskell illustrates, opposite the table of contents to *History and Its Images*, a charming print of a ploughman throwing up his hands in amazement as a pot of coins is revealed in the field where he is at work (Haskell, vi). The scene is not dated, but similar events took place at regular intervals throughout the sixteenth, seventeenth, and eighteenth centuries, especially in areas like the Roman campagna, which were rich in classical remains. Together with the abundant harvest of objects that was customarily found when new foundations were laid in the city of Rome itself, these adventitious treasure troves formed the stock in trade of the original "antiquarians": that is to say, the Roman dealers who sold historical pieces of such varying provenance to the local inhabitants and to the tourist trade.

It is not my intention to challenge the fact that such a practice was already time-honored by the middle of the eighteenth century. Indeed, a gradualist approach to the concept of the development of historical-mindedness would see the eighteenth-century antiquarian as varying little from the pattern set up centuries before and the general practice of antiquarianism as reaching its peak in the Romantic period, after which the superior claims of the new professionalized historiography (and the constitution of archaeology as a scientific practice) took the wind out of its sails for good. But this notion of antiquarianism as an immemorial practice that finally yielded up the ghost in an age of heightened professionalism is quite foreign to the line of argument being traced here. I want to argue two things: first of all, that the antiquarian sensibility of the later eighteenth-century was more intense, indeed qualitatively different from that of earlier periods; second, that its effects were much more positive and much more pervasive than the other view would acknowledge. If we are concerned with the full range of historical representation, and with the possibilities of taking a subjective role in relation to the past, then the antiquarian has a vital part to play in heralding the full-blooded historical-mindedness of the Romantic epoch.

But which antiquarian should we consider? The phenomenon was vast in its ramifications, and space exists here only for one, especially persuasive example of an English antiquarian who achieved his most interesting work over just the same period as Goethe was writing his panegyrics of Erwin von Steinbach. Bryan Faussett, Rector of Monk's-Horton and Perpetual Curate of Nackington, in the vicinity of Canterbury, died in 1776. Over the previous few years, however, he had set up the small brick structure housing historical objects and inscriptions that became known as the Faussett Pavilion.[6] The young Goethe used these years to overcome his initial discomfiture at the "monstrous" appearance of Strasbourg Cathedral and to work out a new identification with the German Middle Ages. Bryan Faussett must have been thoroughly familiar with the great English Gothic Cathedral of Canterbury, which lay almost within sight of his family home at Heppington. His passionate interest was aroused, however, by the fragmented and abraded objects that were dug out of the ground, and in one way or another ended up in his possession. These he treated to a special procedure, which went far beyond the mere act of salvaging and preserving the damaged relics of the past. The Faussett Pavilion was constructed in order that they might become visible once again, and a Latin inscription was compiled for each, so that its provenance, its likely significance, and Faussett's role in its recuperation could be placed on record.

It goes without saying that the objects placed on show in the Faussett Pavilion were a very motley group indeed. One was a "bas-relief image," thought by Faussett to be of King Canute, "the Danish king, who, about A.D. 1023, restored the Cathedral church of Canterbury, destroyed by his own people" (Jessup, 7). Although the attribution is now recognized as fanciful, the sculpture itself is considered to be of some importance. Another was the old font of Kingston Church, "thrown out" and "destined for many years to contain pig-food," which Faussett rescued from sacrilege, and the last owners of the pavilion gave back to its church of origin. By contrast, not much could be made, barring Faussett's lyrical description, of the quern-stone, or as he put it, the "stone cover of an ossuary fashioned like a Roman vessel," which had been turned up by the plough in traditional fashion near the Kentish village of

Sibertswold. This had been, as he confessed, attached to a clay burial urn that was "unhappily broken up by the ploughshare and the all too rough hands of the ploughmen" (Jessup, 6). A similar fate had befallen the effigy in Purbeck marble, which Faussett acquired when it had been "long since dug out of the ruins of St. Augustine's Monastery in Canterbury." It was indeed, by the stage at which Faussett added it to the collection in the pavilion, "a mutilated effigy," which required good faith and a certain imagination in the viewer to credit it as the "ancient sepulchral stone of a bishop or some mitred abbot" (contrary to the expectation set up by the reference to a "mitre," the effigy was entirely defective above the neck).

These judgments on the quality of Faussett's objects, and the pedigrees he thought up for them, are, however, immaterial by comparison with the issue that concerns us most, which is the discursive articulation of the antiquarian's relation to the past. Here the original Latin texts have to be quoted, as their very idiosyncrasies point to the curious intensity of expression that Faussett managed to achieve. The "mutilated effigy" of the putative bishop or abbot is conveyed as "TRUNCAM (PROH DOLOR!) FIGURAM," as though Faussett could not suppress the emotion welling up inside him: "For Grief!" intrudes into the objective listing of the collection. Nor is Faussett averse to admitting the modesty, and provisional character, of his little pavilion. The poor effigy has been offered "some sort of refuge" (ASYLUM, QUALE QUALE), and Faussett himself has been "glad" (LUBENS) to provide it. Now it can rest after so many years spent being "thrown from place to place" (MULTIS ANNIS, HIC ILLIC LACTATO).

It may be argued that Faussett's effusive inscriptions are somewhat sentimental in the way that they dramatize the prehistory of the historical object and the author's role in their retrieval. But that is precisely the point. Faussett uses the Latin text to dramatize a subjective relationship to the object that can only be expressed, in general terms, as a "desire for the past." Indeed, where Winckelmann uses discourse to complete the fragmentary *Torso Belvedere* by giving it a vivid mythic presence as the demigod Hercules, Faussett pieces together for the benefit of his recuperated objects a history that is still provisional and lacunary: beyond the possible identification, it is simply the "pastness" of the fragment, its historical otherness, which makes it worthy of retrieval, both in physical and in rhetorical terms. This comes across strongly in the inscription de-

SAXO HVIC SEPVLCHRALI PERVETVSTO
EPISCOPI VEL ABBATIS CVIVSDAM MILITIVE
TRVNCAM(PROH DOLOR)FIGVRAM EXHIBENTE
E RVDERIBVS COENOBII DIVI AVGVSTINI CANTVARIENSIS,
OLIM, VT CREDITVR, ERVTO,
ET POSTEA, MVLTIS ANNIS, HIC ILLIC LACTATO
ASYLVM, QVALE QVALE, LVBENS PRAEBVIT
BRIANVS FAVSSETT,
A.D.
MDCCLXIX.

7. A mutilated effigy interpreted as the figure of a bishop: from the
Faussett Pavilion (1769).

8. The likeness of King Canute: from the Faussett Pavilion (1769).

vised to accompany the head of "King Canute," which should be quoted in full, again with note being taken of the occasional Latin phrase that has its own special flavor:

> That the bas-relief image which you see represents the like-ness of Canute, the Danish king, who, about A.D. 1023, restored the Cathedral church of Canterbury, destroyed by his own people, is indeed very probable, since it was in fact dug out in A.D. 1764 from the middle of a wall, part of

a building likely to have been erected in Norman times, once called the Guest Hall and situated in the monastery of the same church, fallen, broken, and besmeared with chalk (PRONA, MANCA, GYPSOQUE OBLITA).

Whatever it is, Bryan Faussett, in A.D. 1769, inspired by love of antiquity (VETUSTATIS AMORE INCITATUS), has taken care to set it in this place, however unworthy, where it is preserved from oblivion and rougher hands (ABS OBLIVIONE, ET RUDIORIBUS MANIBUS REDEMPTUM). (Jessup, 7–8)

Faussett's modest pavilion demonstrates both the strengths and the weaknesses of the antiquarian attitude. To no one more than him would Nietzsche's comment apply: "All that is small and limited, moldy and obsolete, gains a worth and inviolability of its own from the conservative and reverent soul of the antiquary migrating into it and building a secret nest there" (*UAH*, 18). Nonetheless, it is obvious that such an individual, indeed obsessional activity, designed to appeal primarily to a small group of like-minded antiquarians with whom Faussett was in frequent correspondence, had the potential to become an enterprise of much wider significance. Winckelmann caused people to look afresh at classical sculpture and began to construct its history; but he did not, on the whole, bring new objects into the cultural sphere. Goethe certainly caused people to look afresh at Gothic cathedrals and "older German architecture." But the consequences of his writing lay perhaps more in the establishment of a German cultural identity than in the incitement to look at medieval architecture in its historical context. Faussett can stand in here for a vast network of eighteenth-century antiquarians who conducted their limited and small-scale operations with such resourcefulness and determination that the basis for a more widespread and popular cult of the past was securely laid.

The point may be emphasized by a further comparison. Who could be expected to follow Faussett's hypotheses about the supposed head of King Canute, written in his own highly idiosyncratic Latin? The answer is obviously that Faussett was appealing to his clerical and antiquarian friends, certainly not to the rough ploughmen who had contrived to wreck the Roman ossuary or the inhabitants of Kingston village who had filled their Purbeck marble font with pigswill. Yet less than a century later, A'Beckett's *Comic History of England* could assume such a mass of ill-assorted knowledge about the Danish king who had briefly been king of England that it was

9. King Canute performs on his favorite instrument: John Leech, illustration to the *Comic History of England* (1851–52).

legitimate to seize on small details of the Canute story and, of course, to express them as parody. The figure whom Leech illustrates as *Canute Performing on His Favourite Instrument* bears a small, and no doubt entirely fortuitous, relationship to Faussett's head, with whom he shares a crown of similar design and a suggestion of kindred drapery. But the Canute of Leech and A'Beckett is bound in to a narrative account that artfully simulates the processes of historical reference. As a gloss on the unlikely image, we are told, "A portion of one of Canute's once popular ballads has been preserved, and if the other verses resembled the one that has come down to us, there is no reason to regret that the rest is out of print and that nobody has kept the manuscript" (A'Beckett, 45). There follows a quotation of the king's "queer quatrain," which begins with the line: "Merrily sing the monks within Ely." As A'Beckett reasonably opines, monks are not in fact notable for singing merry songs, and (here he passes to a footnote) "some writers have endeavoured to justify the royal writer . . . by saying that in those days 'merry' meant 'sad' " (A'Beckett, 46). The satirical intent is, as always, delicately maintained through the persistent exploitation of the conventions of scholarship. Some historians will seriously tell us that, in their period, "black means white," and we will believe them, because this is history.

◆

The purpose of this chapter on the subjective relationship to the past will by this stage, I hope, be amply clear. I have concentrated on the discursive articulation of that relationship by a number of figures who are, in their very different ways, precursors of the empathetic relationship to the past that characterized the Romantic movement. The brief comparison from A'Beckett's *Comic History* is a reminder, however, of the skills in dealing with historical material that had been acquired by the middle of the nineteenth century. It remains for us to look more intensively at the modes of representation developed in the period from 1815 onwards and to examine the creative and rhetorical powers put to the service of the new ideal of "staging the past." After this, it will be necessary to look at a further, more intense development of subjectivity, which has its roots in the early part of the century but flowers most surprisingly towards its conclusion: what can legitimately be called "living the past."

But this transition from subjectivity to the diverse modes of representation (and eventually to the absorption of the subject in representation) should not be allowed to conceal the fact that the type of analysis with which we have just been concerned could well be extended to some of the major figures of the Romantic period. Just as historicism helped to create, in Ranke, the mythic figure of the historian as a person without subjectivity, dedicated solely to the objective ideal of realizing the truth of the past, so Romanticism established in Sir Walter Scott the no less potent myth of a creator who could retrieve past ages for the benefit of the mass reading public, while by no means foregoing the devices of fiction and the instruments of style. To my knowledge, the visual records of Ranke are not specially abundant and do not appear to have been in demand by the public that read his histories. By contrast, the successive portraits of Scott form a fascinating record, both of the differing stages of his life as an author and country gentleman and of the iconographic stereotypes the various painters used to convey his status as the definitive explorer of the rich territory of the past.

In the absence of Ranke, it is useful to take the other German figure of comparable significance in the rediscovery of the past, his compatriot Hegel, for a brief but illuminating visual comparison. In a lithograph dating from 1828, Julius Ludwig Sebbers provided a fascinating image of *Hegel in His Workroom*. The philosopher sits as if half-turned to an audience, with right hand raised as if in an expository gesture, though the eyes are fixed on a far distant point. A black velvet beret (still preserved sedulously in the Hegel birthplace in Stuttgart) protects his head, and otherwise his costume appears to consist of a capacious lined dressing gown, worn over a waistcoat and shirt. The scene is obviously a study, and the books and papers are informally littered here and there, with "PLATO" being visible on the spine of the most prominent. In keeping with this classical text, the decor is uniformly neoclassical in style, from the pedimented bookshelf in the background to the elegant writing chair, whose style distantly recalls the interest aroused in the culture of ancient Egypt by the young General Bonaparte's campaigns. Hegel, in other words, is presented as a thinker, a philosopher working in the great tradition of the Greeks, and not a hint of any antiquarian or Germanic interest obtrudes in the perfect decorousness of the neoclassical interior.

Sir Walter Scott in His Study (Castle Street, Edinburgh), by the Scottish painter Sir John Watson Gordon, is by contrast a much more heterogenous and undeniably complex image. For one thing, it appears to depict the writer in the "den" of his Edinburgh house, which he had left for the splendid new baronial mansion of Abbotsford by the early 1820s, and yet it refers to him as "Sir," when the baronetcy that gave him the right to this title had not been gazetted until 1820. Furthermore, it appears, as a print, in the edition of engraved illustrations to Scott's novel, *The Pirate*, which was published by the Royal Association for the Promotion of the Fine Arts in Scotland in 1871. Watson Gordon is recorded in J. G. Lockhart's *Life of Sir Walter Scott* as having completed an "excellent half-

10. Dressed for philosophical study: L. Sebbers, *Hegel in His Workroom* (1828).

11. Each object has its own story: Sir John Watson Gordon, *Sir Walter Scott in His Study* (1871 print).

length portrait" of the writer in March 1830.[7] But this is certainly not the original for the 1871 engraving we have here. As opposed to Sir William Allan's portrait, *The Author of Waverley in His Study,* which dates from the year before Scott's death in 1832, Watson Gordon's work appears to be an attempt to represent him at the height of his creative powers, and before his historical sense had acquired a concrete and definitive expression in the great construction of Abbotsford.

Here then is Scott as the author of a discourse, and the properties surrounding him have been carefully set on stage to suggest the variety of the points of identification that engage him. He is about to write, the paper in front of him and the pen in his right hand, but his attention is temporarily engaged by the book, or manuscript, which he steadies with his left. Lockhart's *Life* assures us that the decor for Scott's writing was indeed very similar to this: the substantial desk we see in the engraving is "the massive piece of furniture" that he had constructed after the model of one seen at Rokeby Park, with drawers on either side "so that an amanuensis might work opposite to him when he chose" (*LWS,* 386). The cat is no doubt the "venerable tom-cat, fat and sleek" whom Lockhart notes as an inhabitant of the "den," and the more alert dog a rather scaled-down version of "the noble Maida," who was wont to "[thump] the door with his huge paw" (*LWS,* 387). But this affectionate animal company, which rather underscores the sense that Scott is just as at home in the outdoor world as in his "sanctum," also serves to point out the lively interest of various other accessories to the imagination.

Beyond the immediate scene of writing desk and domestic animals, there is in fact an emblematic array of the images and objects that fueled Scott's creative work. The portrait over the fireplace is of his mother, Anne Rutherford, of whom he remarked: "If I have been able to do anything in the way of painting the past times, it is very much from the studies with which she presented me" (*LWS,* 444). Below her, on the mantelpiece, are two precious, historical objects—a broad-based silver chalice and a curious boot with a pointed toe, which seems to be retaining in position a necklace or chain. Whether Watson Gordon is recording specific objects from Scott's personal collection is hard to say. But the weapons mounted on the wall do indeed fit in closely with Lockhart's description of the "den," where he noted the presence of "a Highland Target [shield] on either side [of the chimneypiece], and broadswords and dirks (each having its own story) disposed star-fashion around them" (*LWS*, 386).

Each of the weapons has "its own story," and we may infer that this is also true of the chalice, the shoe, and the chain. Each is capable of figuring in the narrative development of a plot that Scott himself will elaborate from the rich texture of preexisting "stories" prompted by the objects themselves: each can be deployed in a historical account that ranges in time and space, beating the bounds of the map of Europe that forms a backdrop to the writer's half-profiled head. But the most surprising property of all, and one whose authenticity is attested by Edwin Landseer's portrait painting of 1824, is the full suit of armor, with lance in hand, which stands to attention behind Scott's back. Here is a mute participant in the scene, which belongs midway between the world of historical objects and the comfortable domestic scene of the writer and his pets. This suit of armor has a pedigree: it was thought at the time (though erroneously) that it had been worn by the tallest man at the concluding battle of the Wars of the Roses, the Battle of Bosworth Field. But a suit of armor is also very nearly a presence: it seems to stand guard over Scott, whereas in effect it is Scott's creative imagination that lends life, and a potential fictional destiny, to it. Watson Gordon is right to take as Scott's companion in this emblematic scene not the humble amanuensis who takes dictation from the other side of the desk but the ambiguous figure who symbolizes both the preexistent materials on which Scott's imagination was nurtured and the literary panache with which he was able to pump them full of new life.

8

Staging the Past

In one of the large colored etchings for A'Beckett's *Comic History of England*, John Leech depicts in uproarious fashion *The Battle of Bosworth Field, A Scene from the Great Drama of History*. Two people in historical costume cross their blunt swords on a theatrical stage. We see the trapdoor, through which sudden entrances and exits are made, quite clearly in front of us. We also see, to the right and left of the stage, costumed soldiers waiting in the wings for their moment onstage: on the left, a figure distinguished by a Yorkist rose on his surcoat is witnessing with alarm the incautious drinking of his companion; on the right, a knot of heavy, jowled Lancastrians (the roses in their case are colored red) wait gloomily for Richard III to conclude his last combat.

This "Scene from the Great Drama of History" is being played out, according to Leech's conceit, literally as a drama. In fact, the concluding battle in the so-called Wars of the Roses, which marked the end of the Middle Ages in Britain and the advent of the Tudor dynasty, is being played out as if it were the conclusion of Shakespeare's play *Richard III*. Leech has picked perhaps the most obvious instance in English historiography where a historical drama, written in accord with the view of the events taken by the victorious Tudors, has virtually taken the place of the original record. Most English people, no doubt, still think it hard not to see the Battle of Bosworth Field in terms of the single combat between the cocky young Welshman, Henry Tudor, whom we see on the left of the stage, and the

12. *A Scene from the Great Drama of History*: John Leech, *The Battle of Bosworth Field*, illustration to the *Comic History of England* (1851–52).

sinister, hunchbacked assassin of the Princes of the Tower, whom we see to the right. So Leech celebrates (and A'Beckett dignifies with a whole sequence of mock-heroic verses) the existence of a historical stereotype. The actors are characterized, certainly, by some feeble attempts at historical costume. But no one is going to expect Scott's suit of armor, reputedly worn by a giant at the very same battle, to come strolling onto the scene and confront his flimsily dressed adversaries. We accept the stereotype, just as we recognize that, after all, this is a version of the events that risks getting in the way of the events themselves.

But this is not simply a critical reminder of the bogus traditions attaching to a specific moment in English history. Leech has cleverly reversed the point of view of the stage, so that instead of gazing at the backdrop, we see the contemporary audience: a startled mother and her equally alarmed little girl, a top-hatted figure somewhat the worse for drink sprawled over the stalls immediately beyond the crossed swords, random spectators of several shapes and sizes, and finally (we suspect) the distinctly grumpy proprietor of the establishment who surveys them from behind the flats, understandably displeased at the poor turnout. To Leech's contemporaries, this must have seemed like a careful, satirically turned essay in social realism. To us, who occupy the impossible viewpoint more than a century later—when the Victorian costumes are hardly less historical in character than the conventional dresses of the warring Yorkists and Lancastrians—it is a further reminder of the intricacy and self-reflexivity of the history of representation. We see the representation of the Victorian public who are themselves watching history in the process of being represented.

In this context, it is obviously not adequate simply to concede that Shakespeare's version of the Battle of Bosworth Field was a myth, which Leech is by implication exposing and which we safely assume to have been replaced by a historically correct and professionally certified version. Or at least it is not adequate to make that assumption if our primary task is to investigate the historical consciousness of the nineteenth century. Leech's point—not only here, but throughout the work—is that historical representation is never neutral, never transparent. This is a point made clamorously by A'Beckett's text, with its account of the battle in the manner of Macaulay's *Lays of Ancient Rome*. But it is made more pungently, and more economically, by Leech's images. A woodblock of Joan of Arc assaulting the walls of Paris says, this is how you may conceive the event to have taken place, not because you have neglected to read all that is written about Joan, but because, having done the required reading, your concern to visualize the Maid of Orleans has to pass by way of specific (and potentially exaggerated) visual codes. A woodblock of William Wallace says, looking to history for historical modes of representation solves no problem, since what we require of the represented figure ("action," "life") is given not by the "authentic" image but by the spectrum of contemporary modes of representation currently available to us.

This point is amplified by the "Scene from the Great Drama of History" that Leech sets up for our posthumous benefit. This is not simply a theater, but the kind of theater that would have been familiar to Leech and his contemporaries. One detail strikes us and reminds us how significant was the difference between theatrical representation in the nineteenth century and the situation in the present day. Along the front of the stage, clearly visible to us, is a row of guttering candles. The light for this combat, in other words, is being provided by a comparatively feeble source, which means that the difference in luminosity between the stage and the auditorium must be comparatively slight.

It is obvious from this example that Leech's "Great Drama" denotes no transhistorical essence but, on the contrary, a specific comparison between the concept of the "staging" of history and the theatrical practice of his own times. But once this has been admitted, it follows also that his metaphorical transposition of the "action" of history ought to be seen in relation to other contemporary modes of scenic representation, which also purported to re-create the past. From the early 1820s onwards, Daguerre's diorama, installed in London and Paris, provided a vehicle of scenic illusionism that far surpassed the paltry light effects of the traditional theater. Using the contrast between a darkened house and a stage flooded with reflected daylight, Daguerre introduced relatively short, time-based performances in the course of which a vividly painted scene—such as the *Ruins of the Chapel of Holyrood* (see figure 16)—was animated by the changing effects of light and shadow, or even swirling mist. Insofar as it provided, for the period immediately preceding Leech's work, a uniquely powerful mode of representation frequently geared to the recreation of specifically historical tableaux, we must surely say that the diorama, too, helps to define the representational space indicated in the "Great Drama of History." We might even imagine that the candlelit theater would be a suitable subject of satire, precisely because its potential for scenic illusionism is so comparatively slight.

Possibilities of this kind will be considered in the course of this argument about the "staging of history." For the moment, however, it is interesting to note a present-day report that shows beyond a doubt that the debate about historical representation is still closely bound up with the issues of lighting, and scenic illusionism, that became current in the Romantic epoch. From a report in *Le Figaro*, dated 20 April 1993, it appears that the cathedral of Notre-Dame, the most highly visited monument in France, is to be comprehensively restored for the first time since the extensive work of Viollet-le-Duc in the mid-nineteenth century. Restoration, of course, is a process necessary for safeguarding the life of a building, but it opens up immediately the kindred question of the cathedral as a representation. How should Notre-Dame appear to the public, given that its role as a focal point for Parisian tourism is by no means limited to the hours when it can be entered and visited?

The two projects under consideration at the time of the press report indicate beyond a doubt that it is not simply a question of lighting up Notre-Dame but of lighting up Notre-Dame according to a particular scenario, in which the cathedral serves as the vehicle for a more or less historical representation. The first project involves "the anchoring of the monument in its environment and takes into account the gardens, the close, the Seine and the bridge": it is, in other words, a means of reinserting the great church into the urban texture and has little historical significance. By contrast, the second project "is particularly concerned with the temporal aspect. It foresees in particular lighting sequences which can be modified in accordance with the inner rhythm of the life of the cathedral . . . The idea is to symbolize a century of construction by the successive lighting of all the parts of the sanctuary from the apse to the west facade."[1] Whether knowingly or not, the second designer is intent on transforming Notre-Dame into an immense diorama—and it is hardly surprising that the ecclesiastical authorities have responded with a reminder that the church is, after all, still a functioning religious building.

It is not difficult to produce contemporary examples of this kind, which show that the issues debated here, in their early nineteenth-century context, recur constantly in the practical (but also ideological) choices of the present-day world. History as representation forms an integral aspect of the "society of the spectacle." Indeed it is naive to suppose that the cathedral of Notre-Dame was ever, in the strict sense, just a building. It always represented and was intended to represent the power of the Christian church and a means of guidance, through texts and images, to the final bliss of the nontemporal world. But the experience of the last two centuries has added a further dimension. It is not enough for Notre-Dame simply to be an old building, or a building restored, and restored again, with the aim of recapturing its pristine splendor. Notre-Dame must also be an actor in its own historical spectacle, as light breaks it down into its component parts and reassembles them in the form of a historical narrative. It is required to speak to us and activate a fantasy of retrieval through representation, which compensates for our sense of the irrecoverable loss of the past.

This, at any rate, would be a reading consistent with the arguments by Foucault already cited here and with the overall thesis of a "desire for History" with which my discussion began. My concept of "staging the past" implicitly takes for granted a thesis of this kind, since the essential precondition of representation is the need to exteriorize in a particular medium images and fantasies to which the subject declares a relationship of desire and lack. How then do I respond to the conventional objection made against Foucault's concept of the "epistemic cut," which is that no conclusive evidence can ever be brought of the historical shift from one overall system of comprehending the world to another? How, in particular, can the unprecedented nature of the historical consciousness of the Romantic epoch be demonstrated, rather than simply asserted? The main part of my strategy, in relation to this insistent question, is obviously to accumulate the instances of historical representation occurring during this period, proceeding from the evidence of the consciousness of new "historical understanding" among the Romantics to the close analysis of patterns of historical reference and symbolization running through the different visual media. But the next example I shall take serves a double function. As well as suggesting some of the intrinsic (and productive) paradoxes in the concept of the "staging of history," it will suggest one way of formulating the issue of the "break" in historical continuity against which the new historical consciousness took its stand.

◆

François-Marius Granet (1775–1849) was a painter of exactly the same generation as Coupin de la Couperie but of a significantly higher reputation and achievement. Born at Aix-en-Provence, where the major museum still bears his name, he arrived in Paris around 1793 and began to frequent the studio of David; according to Etienne Delécluze, he worked in the company of David's pupils, such as Ingres and Girodet, on the premises of the former Monastery of the Capuchin Friars in the Rue Saint-Honoré in Paris, though his own memoirs refer solely to his working in another disused monastery, the Feuillants (near the Tuileries). His first publicly exhibited painting, in any event, was the *Interior of a Monastery*, shown at the Salon of 1799. After this date, he left Paris for Rome, where he remained for the whole period of the Consulate and Empire, receiving the patronage of Napoleon's uncle, Cardinal Fesch, among others. He finally returned to Paris in 1819 and exhibited in the Salon to great acclaim *The Choir of the Capuchin Church, Rome*, dated 1817. The painting had already been sold before it left the studio. But its subsequent popularity meant that Granet was to execute around fifteen individual versions, one of which (like Coupin's Sully) went to the Duchesse de Berry, who was married to the heir to the Bourbon throne.

Granet's fondness for religious buildings as subject matter for his paintings thus extended from his early years until his maturity; one of his last major works before he became *conservateur* at the Louvre and at Versailles was *The Convent of St. Francis of Assisi* (1822). But his *Capuchin Church* is specially important because it is the subject of a particularly revealing entry in his memoirs. It is important to recognize, as a background to the experience that Granet describes, that Napoleon had annexed the Papal states in 1809 and dissolved the Roman religious houses. His visit to the church of Santa Maria della Concezione was therefore strongly colored by the recollection of a religious life that had been abruptly curtailed:

> I searched in vain in the monasteries for the sweet peace I had once possessed. This led me to the monastery of the Capuchins on the Piazza Barberini; but the good Capuchins were no longer there . . . and dust was beginning to take possession of the carved moldings on the handsome wood-work, which only recently had glistened. The central lectern looked already like a piece of furniture in storage, and its huge missals were no longer opened. Despite this solitude, I could still follow in my mind's eye the movements of all the monks . . . the young novices, with their foreheads calm and resigned after bidding the world farewell and . . . the old men, with their severe heads and noble counte-nances on which one discovered the traces of austerity en-graved by time. My spirit was so keenly aroused by all these thoughts that I resolved to do a large painting on this subject.[2]

The account that Granet provides here is exceptionally interesting if we set it in the context of his whole career. From the start, one might say, he was familiar with the fact that, with the onset of the French Revolution, religious communities were being dissolved and their buildings allocated to other purposes. He had himself worked in one, if not two of these locations, and made one of them the subject of his first major painting. He had also been able to visit the Musée des Monuments français of Alexandre Lenoir, itself a rich assembly of ancient works of art that had been saved from the iconoclasm of the revolutionaries and laid out for public display in the former monastery of the Petits-Augustins. Yet he presents his experience in the Capuchin church as if, for the first time, he con-ceived the possibility of recuperating what was lost through the means of representation. His painting would be not simply the

13. The recovery of sweet peace: François-Marius Granet, *The Choir of the Capuchin Church, Rome* (1817).

record of an existing building but an attempt to re-create "the sweet peace I had once possessed." Hence the psychological tonality of the experience (who can doubt that such "sweet peace" is a generalized notion incorporating many aspects of the middle-aged regret for lost youth?) becomes overdetermined by the specific sentiment of a historical loss. To "do a large painting" that recaptures the vanished world of the Capuchin friars—themselves displaying the whole gamut from thoughtful youth to dignified old age—is a necessary and sufficient way of responding to the complex regret for a vanished past.

To interpret the reaction to feeling "emptied of history" in this personal and psychological way is not, I believe, a trivialization of Foucault's thesis. For the question is not simply, at what point, and why, did Granet and his contemporaries conceive of their relation to the past as one of irretrievable dispossession? It is also, and most significantly for our purposes, at what point, and why, did it become possible for this sense to be widely and effectively diffused through the various media of representation? It is perhaps impossible to answer the first question, and perhaps unnecessary, since it is clear that the whole period of the French Revolution and Empire provided constant reminders that the patterns of ancien régime life were being disrupted and replaced for good. But it is more credible that an answer should be sought, and provided, for the second question. In painting the *Capuchin Church*, as he had known it, Granet was at the same time celebrating all the religious buildings that he had known after their communal life had been terminated. More than this, he was celebrating the very fact that, at this historical stage, the past conceived as a separate dimension became an object of fascination and longing. After all, it was easy enough to reinstate monastic communities and restore traditional dynasties. That was precisely what the period of the "Restoration" in France was about. But it was not possible to dismiss the more profound stirrings of unease. If such a thing had happened once, in so searing and uncompromising a way, it could happen again. The reinstatement of prerevolutionary pomp and circumstance was simply a brave performance that distracted people's minds from the revolutionary abyss.

There is good reason to suppose that, in France especially, the years following 1815 were indeed marked by this widespread conviction that the reinstatement of the trappings of the ancien régime was no more than superficial. Fictional characters like Stendhal's

Marquis de la Mole in *The Red and the Black*, no less than statesmen and writers of the period like Châteaubriand, testify to the sense that Restoration politics was merely an insubstantial pageant, and there could be no guarantee against a further lurch into uncharted territory (see Porter and Teich, 246–47). But such a recognition does not diminish the significance of historical representation at this period. On the contrary, it shows why it was judged necessary and why it achieved public success. The fact that Granet's painting, like Coupin's, passed into the Duchesse de Berry's collection shows (if we were in need of any such evidence) that such fascinating, if ambivalent, icons of historical retrieval were valued precisely by those whose lives were devoted, in a real sense, to bringing back the past. In the next chapter, I shall be looking at some of the interesting consequences, for representation, of the starring role that the elder and younger branches of the Bourbon dynasty were obliged to adopt in postrevolutionary France.

About the ambivalence of Granet's *Capuchin Church*, there is, however, a further point to be made, which specifically relates to the concept of "staging the past," as it will be developed here. It is not accidental that Granet's reminiscence concentrates first of all on the furniture and fittings of the disused church: "the handsome woodwork, which only recently had glistened . . . the central lectern [which] looked already like a piece of furniture in storage." To a certain extent, his mission to "do a large painting" can be interpreted as the fulfillment of a wish to polish up that woodwork once again (and in a permanent fashion), to take that lectern out of store and make it the center of an animated throng once more. Nietzsche's "antiquarian" possesses, and at the same time is possessed by, "his ancestors' furniture." Granet, together with the other artists of the "Style Troubadour" with whom he is associated, can perhaps be accused of investing more passion in the historical objects with which their scenes are replenished than with the characters who act out their roles in the implied narrative. This is, however, not to be taken as a merely moralistic objection. The very nature of historical representation implied a deep ambivalence about the relative importance to be accorded to people and objects, some further aspects of which remain to be investigated here.

◆

I am assuming throughout this study that the French and the English experience of the rise of history in the Romantic period formed

111

an integrated whole. It is legitimate to move from one country to the other, comparing and contrasting the different modes of representation: the distinctive position of Bonington, who has an honored place in both national traditions, provides evidence of an interfusion of ideas and practices that has rarely, if ever, been equaled. Never, perhaps, has English (and Scottish) culture seemed so alluring to the French as in this period following the Napoleonic Wars, when their form of government was a constitutional monarchy *à l'anglaise* and Sir Walter Scott peopled the imagination of writers and painters with his historical narratives.[3] Yet it must be emphasized at the same time that the French, veterans of the Revolution and the Empire, experienced the sense of being emptied of history more acutely than the nation that had witnessed the convulsions of Europe from the sidelines. No English artist had an experience of the curtailment of history and tradition comparable with that of Granet or Coupin; no English artist, perhaps, would have felt the need to concretize that feeling in an image as acutely as Granet did with his *Capuchin Church*.

Hence the English antiquarian movement, which was already well established by the latter part of the eighteenth century, preserved well into the Romantic period—and indeed never entirely lost—the querulous, eccentric, and slightly perverse character it had acquired in an age when the determined pursuit of the objects of the past was mainly a pastime reserved for country clergymen and Oxford dons. It was not, as a rule, invested with the deadly seriousness it had acquired for those who spent their early youth as "scribes following the canons" (Prosper de Barante's eloquent phrase).[4] Consequently the examples of historical representation that stand out in this period on the English side of the Channel are characterized by a more profound ambivalence than their French counterparts. This does not mean that they are any less interesting. On the contrary, the very difficulties the English experienced in adjusting their styles to the exigencies of historical representation are highly illuminating from our point of view. Taking for consideration the works of Cotman, who largely failed in his objectives, and Bonington, who largely succeeded, we are able to appreciate very precisely the complex, and often unforeseen, constraints that bore on the project of staging the past.

John Sell Cotman (1782–1842) belongs in the annals of English art as an example of a youthful genius who lost his way. He did so (as the official version goes) precisely through venturing out into antiquarian projects that were too ambitious to succeed and that involved a cavalier neglect for his real talent as an artist in watercolors. Certainly there is no doubt that Cotman's early drawings and watercolors are among the most technically original and aesthetically pleasing works of their period. He possessed a rare ability to match his vision of the outside world with a sensitivity to pictorial construction within the limits of the framing edge that is almost Japanese in its refinement. Only Cotman, among English artists of this period, can give a similarly persuasive structure to both an aqueduct and a drop gate in a park.[5] It is hardly surprising that he also exercised his talents on the historic buildings of his native Norwich and produced some outstanding interiors of its fine Norman cathedral. *Interior of the Nave, Norwich Cathedral* (1807) turns an "ungainly corner" of the building into "one of the most poetic interior pieces he ever did" (*Cotman*, 93). When he represents *Jesus Chapel, Norwich Cathedral* (1807–1880), he is unconcerned by the fact that this chapel was at the time being used "as some sort of lumber room" (*Cotman*, 95). It is indeed grist to his mill that the cathedral's fine medieval pelican lectern should have been shoved in a corner, near a pair of ladders, as this informal placing makes the composition all the more casually effective.

From this brief account, we can surely take it that Cotman's pictorial aims at this stage were as far removed as possible from any project of historical representation, as it has been defined here. Where Granet sought to redeem the lectern of the Capuchin church from its sad condition as "furniture in storage," Cotman accepts that the lectern is precisely that, and succeeds in making a poetic composition out of the incongruity. But the demands of Cotman's career, and the fact that his most active patron was the Norfolk antiquarian, Dawson Turner, conspired to turn his activities more and more in the direction of the representation of antiquities. In 1812 he moved with his family to Yarmouth, which was also Dawson Turner's home. Turning from watercolors, he began to work more and more in the medium of etching, which offered the commercial attraction of multiple editions, to be sold to prosperous subscribers. Cotman was certainly not the first British artist to engage in this newly developing practice of "antiquarian topography" (*Cotman*, 23). But his *Architectural Antiquities of Norfolk* (1812–18) and his *Antiquities of Normandy* (1819–22) are unquestionably among the most ambitious of the genre. The Normandy etchings were the culminating achievement of his career and had involved special expeditions to the continent in 1817, 1818, and 1820.

In what sense was Cotman's *Architectural Antiquities of Normandy* a work of historical representation or, indeed, an attempt at staging the past? The answer to this question is not immediately obvious. What is entirely clear, however, is that the edition of etchings in four magnificent volumes was intended to support his claim to be the leading artist dealing with antiquities after the death of Charles Alfred Stothard in 1821 (*Cotman*, 24). Stothard had begun to issue his great collection of *Monumental Effigies* in 1811, and he had offered a ringing justification for the task of scrupulous recording of monuments that he had set himself: "To history they give a body and a substance, by placing before us those things which language is deficient in describing."[6] No doubt it is true that Stothard's distinctive way of presenting his effigies—showing them from different angles, with fine detail and dramatic shading—does give a vivid impression of the medieval period. They are (as he expressed it in his allegorical frontispiece) "rescued from Time" insofar as they are placed before the reader in such a way as to excite the imagination. But this is an effect that has to be completed by Stothard's own evocative narrative passages, which accompany the fragmented images. Only when we become absorbed in his account of the exciting career of William Longespée, Earl of Salisbury, does the stiff effigy of the great warrior spring to life.

According to this criterion of interdependence between image and text, the *Antiquities of Normandy* is hardly a success. This is because Cotman's admirable patron, Dawson Turner, insists on parading his own antiquarian knowledge in a way that does not complement, and indeed in a sense detracts from, the effect of Cotman's plates. He wishes to appear profoundly familiar with what has been written about the history of Normandy by recent authors. Indeed, to all appearances, he is extremely well read in the area. But this leads him to affect an ostentatious and pedantic display of learning, of which this prefatory remark is a fair specimen: "Whoever can take pleasure in the wildest extravagancies of absurd fiction, displayed in theories destitute of even the slender basis of tradition, yet raised with plausibility, connected with ingenuity, and supported by learning, may find abundant gratification in the early history of Falaise."[7]

14. Antiquarian topography: John Sell Cotman, *Mount St Michel, The Knights' Hall*, from the *Architectural Antiquities of Normandy* (1819–22).

It may be wondered precisely what relation Cotman's etchings have to this extravagant and self-glorifying discourse. The answer must surely be that Cotman is an accurate draftsman and that his careful renderings of the interiors and exteriors of the historical locations to which Turner refers succeed in providing a kind of "reality effect" to authenticate the antiquarian's claims. When Turner comes to describe the early history of the Mont-Saint-Michel, he is supremely contemptuous of the legends that have gathered to cloud the accounts of the pre-Conquest epoch, but assures us that from 1066 onwards, "History . . . assumes a character of comparative authenticity" (*Normandy*, 4:117). His account of one of the interiors on the Mont-Saint-Michel, which is the subject of a Cotman etching, simply enumerates the bare facts about the building, which we can then verify (if we feel so inclined) by checking Cotman's image for ourselves: "The Knights' Hall, see *plate ninety-six*, is an arched chamber, ninety-eight feet in length, by sixty-eight in width, noble and church-like in its aspect. Its groined stone roof rests upon eighteen cylindrical columns, with bases and capitals; the latter, in very high relief, of beautiful design and delicate execution" (*Normandy*, 4:121).

It is perhaps unfair to stigmatize poor Dawson Turner for his extravagant and redundant comments, especially when it appears that Cotman himself was instrumental in persuading him to provide them. Is it not obvious that Cotman aspired precisely to the aim of "antiquarian topography," and nothing more than this? Was he not concerned just to show what was there? The fact that he used a camera lucida projecting device to record architectural elevations on his first tour of Normandy in 1817 suggests a desire for accurate specification above all else.[8] There is even some evidence to suggest that Cotman's problems with his eyesight were leading him, as early as 1814, to employ assistants and "perhaps to develop a more mechanical technique which could be easily imitated by others" (*Cotman*, 25). Is it then surprising that the Normandy etchings should have been a commercial failure and that Cotman himself should have forthwith abandoned antiquarian work? How seriously, in consequence, should we treat the whole enterprise?

The answer to this question can only be forthcoming if we look more closely at the images themselves, that is to say, at the very property that differentiates them from Dawson Turner's redundant passages of description. There may be "eighteen cylindrical columns" in Cotman's etching of the "Knights' Hall," but they are distributed in accord with the single viewpoint of a monocular perspective. As with those enigmatic architectural perspectives of the Quattrocento, which Hubert Damisch has memorably analyzed, these interiors appear to offer nothing but the extension of a methodically constituted space. Yet their very constitution, however much it depends on the aid of mechanical instruments like the camera lucida, is a form of statement; as Damisch puts it, "Perspective is not a code; but it has in common with language the fact that, in it and by it, is instituted or constituted, by means of a point, an instance analogous to that of the 'subject' in language, of the 'person,' always placed in relation to a 'here' or a 'there,' with all the possibilities of passing from one position to the other which derive from that."[9] Cotman does not simply "describe" the Knights' Hall. He stages the coming into discourse of a space, from the position of one who sees. This apparently trivial point is, as we shall see, crucial in establishing Cotman's relationship to the later forms of documentation considered here.

If perspective is not a code but a form of statement or "enunciation," what about luminosity, which is the vehicle through which Cotman cunningly diversifies and establishes his interior space? In a sense, luminosity is both a "code" and a "mode," to use Umberto Eco's snappy formulation.[10] It is a mode to the extent that different patterning and intensification of the etcher's line creates the range of tonalities from the almost white to the almost black, which we read as light and shadow. In the unique copy of the full set of different states of the Normandy images, which is preserved in the British Museum, we can see Cotman going over the plate again and again to achieve richer and darker shadows (the illustration used here is an early state, and consequently much more luminous than its successors). But obviously, since "antiquities" are involved, the code of light and dark is not simply a matter of technical registration. The "historical" character of the buildings is much enhanced by the presence of velvety shadows, and, correspondingly, the first states of the etchings seem to lack any compelling power to evoke the memory of the past.

This point is underscored if we compare Cotman's strategy in the *Knights' Hall* etching with one of the finest of the whole series, which has understandably been singled out and exhibited out of context. The *Knights' Hall* plate makes no bones about the fact that this is a contemporary image of a historical building. A soldier stands at the end of the room, marking its length in a way that is familiar from innumerable Dutch church interiors. Another soldier is seated on the left, engaged in conversation with a seated figure. What kind of soldiers are these? It is at least conceivable that they are English soldiers, since the Duke of Wellington led an English force of occupation that did not leave French soil until 1817. But, even if they are French, their presence marks the view of the Knights' Hall in a way that is slightly ironic: they are, after all, so different, in their uniform and their relaxed demeanor, from what we might have expected of the original knightly company.

By contrast, Cotman's *Crypt of the Abbey Church of the Holy Trinity at Caen* (from the second volume) is richer and darker and excludes any human presence. Cotman has exploited the fact that the crypt is underground and receives natural light from only one corner to set up a sumptuous pattern of minutely varied marks that conveys the different intensities of shadow. He has, moreover, included to the left of the composition, in the place that is equivalent to the soldier and his mate's position in the Knights' Hall, two broken Romanesque capitals, one of which lies wrong side up on the stone floor, and the other of which sits right side up on a small ledge. The fact that no human presence invades this subterranean space makes it much more potent as an evocation of the past: the twin capitals, however, suggest a discreet allegory of the contemporary attitudes to medieval architecture in this period. Cotman does not assume a subjective relationship to the medieval building in its entirety (as Goethe does); nor does he seize on the stray stone in order to invest it with an antiquarian passion (like Bryan Faussett); his almost casual incorporation of the two capitals that help his composition suggests at the same time the possibility of a discourse of restoration and rehabilitation. It is as if the image were telling us that these seemingly disregarded fragments would be put back in a place of honor if those who have charge of them looked at the Abbey Church with the same degree of fidelity as the engraver has.

Cotman's *Architectural Antiquities of Normandy* is a bran tub from which curators and collectors pick the odd striking plate, mindful usually of the fine sense of pictorial structure, which, in a number of cases, causes these etchings to be reminiscent of his earlier work. Not much attention is given to the enterprise as a whole. Yet this is understandable, since Cotman's hard work and high ambition for the series was not matched by a thorough self-awareness about what was being undertaken. Considered as historical representation, the work as a whole is perhaps a hybrid. Dawson Turner's antiquarian flourishes introduce a discourse in which the mythic element in historical tradition is exposed to merciless sarcasm and the virtue of the modern approach is officiously demonstrated. The merit of Cotman's images lies, at least in part, in their scrupulous, measurable accuracy. But what purpose does the accuracy serve? Given that perspective is a form of enunciation, one might put the critical case that this is a purely neutral enunciation—a statement about nothing—except insofar as the developing historical culture of the times enriches it with connotations. Like John Cage, Cotman states: I have nothing to say, and I am saying it, and that is poetry. And so it is, after a fashion.

To put the case for (or against) Cotman in this way is to be mindful of the exactly contrary case that can be made for the younger British artist, Richard Parkes Bonington (1802–36). Despite the brevity of his career, Bonington had the advantage of catching the full tide of the Romantic movement; indeed, few, if any other, artists in England or in France have as good a claim to have understood the possible implications for representation of history. In contrast to Cotman, who toiled to obtain the best results from the recalcitrant medium of etching, Bonington was able to exploit the new media and test their capacity for serving as vehicles for the evocation of the past. It is surely no accident that his first major production in this area took as its subject matter the very same general subject matter that Cotman had painstakingly researched from 1817 onwards. The set of ten lithographs he produced in 1823–24 carried the title *Restes et fragmens d'architecture du moyen âge, recueillis dans diverses parties de la France et dessinés d'après nature par R. P. Bonington* (Remains and fragments of medieval architecture, collected in various parts of France and drawn after nature by R. P. Bonington). But the subtitle is "Little Normandy"—"La petite Normandie." Interest in Normandy as the part of France most closely associated with English history over a long period was undoubtedly high in the years of the French Restoration. It was to be fostered on the French, as well as the British, side of the Channel by the publication of Augustin Thierry's *Histoire de la Conquête de l'Angleterre par les Normands* in 1825. But it can hardly be doubted that one of Bonington's motives for working in this domain was his awareness of the precedent of Cotman's series.

Of special significance in gauging the novel effect of Bonington's "Little Normandy" is the choice of lithography, rather than etching, for his medium. Lithography had been invented towards the end of the previous century in Bavaria and made little headway in France until the period of the Restoration. In 1818, however, Charles Nodier, who was on an archaeological trip to Normandy, conceived the idea of making use of the new technique for the systematic record of architectural antiquities. This was not only because of its comparative cheapness, judged against traditional engraving on metal plates, but because the lithographic stone offered the possibility of striking new effects. Nodier conceived the potentiality of the lithograph primarily as one of re-creating the freshness and immediacy of the traveler's experience. As he put it, "the bold pencil of the lithograph seems to have been invented to fix the free, original and rapid inspirations of the traveller who gives an account of his sensations."[11] Nodier's idea of using lithography in this way was to bear fruit in the 1820s in the immensely successful collective project of the *Voyages pittoresques et romantiques dans l'ancienne France*, in which Bonington was one of the many collaborators.

Yet Bonington brings a distinctively new element to the topographical lithograph. In his case, there is certainly visual evidence of the "bold pencil," and a sense of spontaneous delight in the flexibility of the medium. But this is doubled by a project that Bonington understood better than any of his contemporaries: that of staging the past. Even the rejected title page for his "Little Normandy" series makes this clear. We see a doorway in the most splendid flamboyant Gothic style: two charmingly posed small boys are grouped to one side, their attention being taken by a large dish or charger (so it appears) that lies at the bottom of the steps that offer access. As in the striking *Knight and Page*, extremely clever use is made of the establishment of successive planes. Where the page in the oil painting jauntily places his foot on the level occupied by the knight, the two Norman urchins are arranged so that one perches on a low step and the other stands next to him, fixing his gaze on the charger. We as spectators, however, follow the sequence of worn steps until they curve round out of sight, and our gaze is met by the exceptionally simple, limitlessly evocative plane of a blank wall. *Restes gothiques* (Gothic remains) is the suggestive title of this inauguratory image, which gives nothing away but precisely leads us to the very threshold of a new space to be discovered and whets our appetite for the further images to be shown.

Fundamental to Bonington's creative use of lithography was his desire to use special papers and "tint stones" (stones already possessing a ground colour) in the achievement of his effects. The French printer Feillet, to whom "Little Normandy" was entrusted, used three different types of paper for this print, including a "white paper with a tobacco-brown tint stone then being tested for deluxe editions of Baron Taylor's *Voyages pittoresques*" (Noon, 103). The excellent possibilities offered by this new support for the medium can be judged from observing the way in which the tint stone has been used in Bonington's ninth plate for the "Little Normandy" series: *Entrée de la Salle des Pas-Perdus, Palais de Justice, Rouen.* Based on drawings of this spectacular late Gothic building, which Bonington had accumulated since 1821, this print achieves a fine balance between the meticulous and delicate drawing of the *flamboyant* detail and the soft, broad effects of light and shadow, playing across the stonework and the massive roof. The golden glow produced by the "tobacco-brown" tint has something of the same evocative power as the sepia tonality of certain old photographs (as opposed to the more conventional black and white). We register the image not only as an accurate record, designed to satisfy antiquarian interest, but as a "shifter" (to use the linguist Jakobson's term) between present and past.

This is attested by the fact that Bonington has played a cunning

15. A shifter between present and past: Richard Parkes Bonington, *Palais de Justice, Rouen,* from *Restes et fragmens* (1823–24).

game with the spectator, or reader, of the print. He provides his usual cherished motif of the flight of steps, evocative of a further space we can approach by stages but only penetrate finally through the imagination. Down these steps are proceeding lawyers dressed in ceremonial garb, as is appropriate for a Palais de Justice. But is this in fact a contemporary scene (that is, set in the 1820s), or is it a historical re-creation? As we scan the groups of people massed around the steps, we can see that some are indeed wearing traditional dress still used in the contemporary period (for example, the two friars on the left), but others are undoubtedly garbed in the short cloaks and feathered hats of the sixteenth or seventeenth century. The more we look, the more this variegated chorus that appears onstage against the backdrop of the historic building turns out to be a representation of the past life of the city of Rouen. Unlike

Cotman's post-Napoleonic soldiers, lounging in the Knights' Hall, these figures are part of an integral imaginative projection (or retrojection); they mark the building itself as belonging, mysteriously, to two separate time scales, which are reconciled in the technical achievement of the tint-stone lithograph.

Bonington was not always authorized to play fast and loose with the conventions of topography in this way. When he was commissioned to provide a plate on the *Rue du Gros-Horloge, Rouen* for the volume of the *Voyages pittoresques* published in 1824, he contented himself with showing this populous city street crowded with the contemporary inhabitants (some, admittedly, in traditional peasant dress). But such a work is nonetheless "a masterwork of romantic lithography" (Noon, 108), because of Bonington's exceptional sensitivity to the possibilities of the new medium. Where the engraver must necessarily rely for his effects on the bitten line, a lithographer like Bonington can combine the soft fluency of the pencil with a magical quality of the delicate ground (in this case, a *chine collé*, that is to say, a paper covered with a bonded layer of wafer-thin tissue). But Bonington's Rouen street scene is remarkable not only for its silvery and intricate surface texture. It also adopts a "plunging perspective" that concentrates attention on the monument that gives the street its name, the "Gros Horloge," or belfry. To have combined the values of such sensitive surface treatment with a boldly distorted perspective that at the same time focuses on the presiding monument of the scene is a full measure of Bonington's ingenuity and verve. It was in fact comparatively rare for the many artists who contributed to the *Voyages pittoresques* to take such expressive liberties (Noon, 108).

It has been pointed out that Bonington's initiative in choosing to accentuate the effect of perspective makes his work comparable with the scenographic procedures of the diorama. If we look at the painting Daguerre completed in 1824, as a prelude to his diorama on the same subject shown in London in 1825–26, we can certainly see the similarity. Daguerre was himself a contributor to the *Voyages pittoresques*. But this large and bold oil painting obviously relates more closely to the scenographic display of the diorama, with its dramatic changes of light against the gaunt profile of the Gothic building, than it could to any modest realization of the printmaker. The diorama was by no means confined to historical subject matter, and relying as it did on painted flats that were enlivened by sequences of shifting light, it could not count (like Bonington's Rouen

16. The Gothic ruin brought to life by light: Daguerre, *Ruins of the Chapel of Holyrood* (1824).

prints) on the animated effect of onstage crowds in period or con-temporary dress. But it was well designed to convert the experience of the dominant "view"—already well established in Western cul-ture as a result of developments in painting and garden design in the eighteenth century—into an imaginative experience of the historical domain. The Chapel of Holyrood might be ruined and desolate. But a public which had become familiar with the life of Mary Queen of Scots, from the drama of Schiller or the novels of Sir Walter Scott, could allow its own prior knowledge to color the spectacle.

This dual pertinence of the diorama, which presents the objects to a maximum degree of visibility but at the same time offers them as tokens of knowledge, is effectively demonstrated by a bill adver-tising the Regent's Park program towards the end of the 1820s.[12] On one side of the advertisement there is a description of the "View of Paris from Montmartre / painted by Daguerre." On the other there is publicity for a "Historical description of the Campo Santo of Pisa / painted by Bouton." As detailed in the latter: "The tombs, altars, vases and fragments of architecture which follow, nearly all belong to the most remote ages, and present, notwithstanding their mutilated state, an historical interest." Where the *View of Paris from Montmartre* offers well-known landmarks and buildings to be seen and identified, the image of the Campo Santo provides a more nebulous prospect and a greater test for the imagination; nonetheless, the guarantee of "historical interest" is there for any members of the public who might be disconcerted by the "mutilated state" of the objects, and they also have the satisfaction of knowing that their effort of understanding is being paralleled by a concerted attempt to restore the dilapidated ambiance. "This monument, which had long been abandoned, is now undergoing repairs calculated to preserve the sepulchral tombs of which it is the depository."

"Staging the past" is, in a more literal way than with any of the media hitherto discussed, the stated aim of at least one type of diorama. And it does so in conditions very different from Leech's *Great Drama of History*; not with the uncertain light of a few guttering candles but with a darkened house and a stage flooded with spectacular illumination. But the diorama is not, of course, the definitive answer to the problem of historical representation. It can evoke the Campo Santo or the Chapel of Holyrood. But its intelligibility and imaginative appeal are dependent, in that process, on the extent to which they make use of the knowledge already acquired through the audience's desire for history. Equally, it can adapt the distorted perspectives of architectural draughtsmen in order to make the illusion of presence even more striking from the spectator's point of view. But it cannot ally that effect of perspective, as Bonington could, with a treatment of surface that gives equal attention to luminosity and to fine, intricate detail. It can try to integrate the display of the historical object with the social demand for strategies of restoration and conservation, as Cotman may have aspired to do. But it cannot equal Cotman, let alone Bonington, in implying that the object or scene has a double existence, shifting from past to present in the very strangeness of its material identity.

As is only too well-known, however, the diorama was only one stage in the inventive and fertile career of Louis-Jacques-Mandé Daguerre, who was participating in the experiments of Nicéphore Niepce before the close of the 1820s, and went on to develop the daguerreotype by the end of the next decade. It is easy to be proleptic about the history of photography in the nineteenth century. Indeed, it is almost impossible not to see the various changes in the technology of representation with which we have been concerned in this chapter—from etching to lithography, from theatre to diorama—as having a premonitory role in creating the conditions for photography. As Fox Talbot put it, photography is the "pencil of light," softer than the engraver's tool—softer even than the lithographer's pencil—and able to combine the finest registration of detail with the utmost fidelity of ambient light. Yet if we look at the development of photography from the point of view of historical representation, the status of the photographic image is not entirely clear. In terms of our original distinction between *discours* and *histoire*, it must surely be argued that the photograph does not provide the possibility for the discursive articulation that has been the guiding thread in this series of examples. The photograph is *histoire* and not *discours*, even though the photographer may invent a second-order discourse in which it has a part to play. Barthes's contrast between the "purely intellectual discourse" of history and photography as "a sure testimony, but a fleeting one" is too broad for the concerns of this study.[13] But if we insert the rider that history can be a "poetic" as well as a "purely intellectual" discourse, the antithesis is still valid.

We cannot, however, dismiss the photograph as easily as that from this discussion of "staging the past," or indeed from historical representation in general. For the moment, let it be taken that the photograph indicates a kind of vanishing point for the discourses examined here: it is precisely that point at which the object and the representation become coincident, and there is no need for staging. The enunciatory role of perspective and the coding of luminosity with regard to surface are negated, in the same measure as they are achieved mechanically by the photographic process. Yet this vanishing point, this annulment of discourse and scenography, is already inscribed within the historical representation of the 1820s: it is there, if only as a Utopian ideal, and a few significant, though aberrant examples testify to it.

In the second volume of Cotman's *Architectural Antiquities of Normandy*, there is an etching that stands out from all the others. It does not represent an architectural interior or an external view of a monument. It is flat, with an alternating pattern of Latin script and finely textured surfacing, and Cotman has, quite exceptionally, provided precise dimensions for its extent in both directions. This

17. Replication without representation: John Sell Cotman, *Fac simile of the Inscription upon the Tomb of Queen Matilda*, from the *Architectural Antiquities of Normandy* (1819–22).

is, as Cotman's inscribed writing at the bottom of the image tells us, *A Fac Simile of the Inscription upon the Tomb of Queen Matilda in the Abbey Church of the Holy Trinity at Caen*. In Dawson Turner's text, there is further elucidation of the way in which this unusual image came to be included:

> The engraved stone in *plate twenty-six*, marks the place which [Queen Matilda's tomb] occupies. Upon it is laid the original slab with the epitaph, which, by great good fortune, escaped unhurt from the hands both of democrats and Huguenots; and, as many of the subscribers to this work have expressed a desire that a fac-simile of it should be inserted, as illustrative of the form of the letters, as well as of the manner of writing in use at that period, Mr Cotman has had a pleasure in meeting their wishes, at the same time, that he has not considered it as sufficiently belonging to the publication, to justify him making it an object of charge. (*Normandy*, 2:35)

In a double sense, this "fac-simile" plate escapes the economy of Cotman's enterprise: first, by being a bonus for the lucky subscribers, and second, by being set within no spatial context that would establish it as an object. The "original slab" is, as it were, transcribed for the benefit of Cotman's erudite antiquarian public. And yet it is not simply transcribed, because the subscribers are interested in the "form" and "manner" of the text: what we see is therefore a kind of replica, or transfer, corresponding to the instruction *fac simile*—make like! Throughout the nineteenth century, and similarly in a domain reserved for antiquarians and bibliophiles, the notion of the "fac-simile" continues to develop, until by the 1880s Elliott Stock is issuing "fac-simile reprints" of seventeenth-century texts like Izaak Walton's *The Complete Angler*. By this stage, as we are told in the preface to the latter re-edition, the original types, woodcuts, and title page "have been reproduced by a photographic process which is simply infallible; and the publisher has not neglected any available mechanical means to secure an absolute *fac-simile* of the original book."[14]

Replication without representation—it is easy to see why such a concept and practice developed within a culture that was permeated with the desire for history. Barante's ambition to let the medieval chroniclers speak for themselves and Ranke's determination to use

18. A print from the seventeenth century, or a photograph from the
nineteenth? Niépce, photoengraving of print of the Cardinal
d'Amboise (1827).

nothing but original sources here find their visual equivalent in the notion of an unmediated registration of the reality of the past. Cotman, of course, is cheating: his "slab," which espouses the flatness of the page, is nonetheless an etching, produced by the same laborious process as all the others (though without the calculations of perspective). But, just a few years after Cotman's edition, the Frenchman Nicéphore Niépce perfects a process that will, to his satisfaction, reproduce the effects of lithography without testing the drawing skills of the artist in charge. His "photoengraving" of a print of the Cardinal d'Amboise, originally dated 1650, faithfully picks up the rough cross-hatching and dark tones of the earlier work: it does so, however, by utilizing the automatic registration of light on a photosensitive surface. With a strictly practical and commercial end in view, Niépce is engaged in the process that will eventually lead to him being acknowledged as the first practitioner of photography. His partner, Daguerre, will use the decade of the 1830s in further experiments to ensure the best possible conditions for the automatic registration of light. With the wide publicity given to his personal invention, the daguerrotype, by the French Academy of Sciences in 1839, the photograph comes of age.

9

Living the Past

Niepce's photoengraving of the Cardinal d'Amboise produces the equivalent of a dizzying sensation in the mind. What period does it belong to? The heavy paper support and the dense, textured effect of the image seem to tell us that this is not a nineteenth-century replica but an original print from the cardinal's own period. It certainly bears no relation to the daguerreotype, bonded to its thin slab of copper, or to the fragile paper mounting of Fox Talbot's calotypes. Yet this is an image from 1827. And if it is hard to imagine it as a kind of protophotograph, it is not difficult to see it as the product of a compelling desire to explore the reality of the past through representation, even to the point where the act of representation itself is replaced by means of a cunning chemical subterfuge. The historians, in their self-proclaimed desire to reach the truth of the original sources, had at least the advantage that they would not be upstaged by the discovery of a process that enabled the evidence to "speak for itself." But in the broader field of historical representation, as in the area of visual art in general, the photograph testified to an impossible moment of coincidence between past and present: it did not annihilate representation, but it undoubtedly raised the stakes.

There has been a general recognition for some time that the effect of photography on painting was precisely to impel painters to accentuate those properties the photograph did not possess: if the oil painting could not compete with the photograph's registration of light, it could capitalize on the resources of color (unavailable to the photographer until after 1900) and on the animation of the surface through distinctive use of the brush. What I shall argue is that the effect—not perhaps of photography in itself but of the desire for the real of which photography provided the most unambiguous sign—was to make the objective of "staging the past" no longer an adequate goal. In the materials that formed the subject matter of Chapter 8, historical objects, ranging from a lectern to a memorial slab, were given an enhanced identity through representation. But the further possibility remains to be investigated. To what extent was it possible not simply to "stage the past" but to "live the past"? Did the data of history offer a sufficiently rich potential for identification on a personal and psychological level, as well as through the medium of the object?

In a real sense, we risk neglecting the importance of this question because we know the end of the story all too well. A photograph on the front page of my morning newspaper shows what are to all intents and purposes soldiers from the American Civil War, in uniforms from the Union and Confederate sides. It is just possible that this might be a historical record of the war itself, since the American Civil War was indeed one of the first to be extensively documented by photography. These individuals with grizzled beards, standing casually behind a collection of their weapons, could have been photographed at the time, although the oblique, close-up pose has little in common with the more formal documentation of the nineteenth-century war photographer. Yet, unlike the Niepce *Cardinal d'Amboise*, this does not really provoke a frisson of indecision as to which time signature it bears. There is no difficulty whatsoever in assuming that these people are actually playing war games. The newspaper caption explains: "The American Civil War Society handed over their Springfield rifles to the Imperial War Museum yesterday for safe keeping while they saw the sights of London. At Eastnor Castle in Herefordshire at the weekend the American enthusiasts will re-enact the Union victory at the battle of Antietam in 1862."[1]

If we were not so inured to ceremonials of this kind, we might reflect on the extraordinary plasticity of the historical imagination as it is revealed in this extract. To operate as soldiers of the American Civil War, these "enthusiasts" have no need of an original frame, or scenography.

They can reenact the battle of Antietam at Eastnor Castle, which cannot be a very credible substitute. Anything "historical" will do, no doubt, for this specific recreation, just as anything warlike will take their off-duty interest, witness the visit to the Imperial War Museum. But the realms of museology and historical reenactment do just intersect, to the extent that they visit in uniform (but without their Springfield rifles) the educational repository of the accumulated war relics of the British Empire.

This little incident prompts a more far-reaching question. At what stage, and in what circumstances, did the practice of dressing up in "historical" clothes and "reenacting" the past become current? This practice may be distinguished from the acting of historical drama, which exists securely within representation, or indeed from the type of "reenactment" presupposed in ceremonies like the coronation of a king or the enthronement of an archbishop, however much (as we shall see) these cultural conventions turn out to be closely associated with it. What I am asking is when, if at all, the motif of historical recreation—"living the past"—can be effectively disentangled from the concepts of dramatic representation, ceremony, and even ideology in such a way that a pure (and distinctively Romantic) element emerges.

Perhaps the most well-known account that tells of a process recognizably similar to this (though from the Renaissance rather than the Romantic epoch) is the letter in which the exiled Niccolò Machiavelli describes the life he leads in his Tuscan farm of San Casciano:

> When evening is come, I return to the house, and enter my study; and on the threshold I put off this daytime dress, full of mud and dirt, and put on my royal and curial robes; and decently accoutred, I enter the ancient courts of the men of old, where I am welcomed kindly by them, and feed on that fare which is mine alone, and for which I was born: where I am not ashamed to speak with them, and ask them the reasons for their actions; and they reply in their humanity; and for four hours I feel no cares, I know no more trouble, I do not fear poverty, death loses its terrors for me: I am entirely transferred into them [*tucto mi tranferisco in loro*].[2]

Machiavelli's celebrated letter describes with exceptionally clear detail a process of "dressing up" in historical clothes, with the effect that modern scholars have debated the issue of "what did Machiavelli wear in the country?"[3] It is indeed fascinating to speculate on what he may have meant by the "panni reali e curiali" in which he encountered the classical authors with whom he was in dialogue. Without any doubt, it can be said (in terms of the criteria used in this study) that Machiavelli conceived of history as a *discours*, and not as *histoire* alone. His *Discorsi*, written as the result of the period of exile from Florence, took the form of a systematic interrogation of the sources for Greek and Roman history, which he carefully evaluated in the search for lessons to be applied in the current circumstances. So Machiavelli writes discursive history, and his relation to the past is (in Nietzsche's terms) overridingly monumental. But this recognition does not solve the problem of the clothes.

Two antithetical possibilities seem to define the limits of any interpretation of Machiavelli's passage. On the one hand, he is simply using a vivid figure of speech: to dress "in royal and curial clothes" is a way of saying that Machiavelli prepared himself for the solemn experience of reading in his study, just as being "transferred into them" implies being absorbed in the intellectual dialogue. On the other hand, Machiavelli is referring to a real costume, reminiscent of antiquity, which he put on as he entered his sanctum. Perhaps the solution to the question lies between these two stark alternatives. In all events, it is obvious that our sense of what is implied in putting on the clothes of the past is irretrievably colored by a tradition of using historical costume in drama, painting, and other modes of representation that have accumulated since Machiavelli's time. What we do know about Machiavelli's encounter with the classical historians is that it was not the "pastness" of the past, but precisely its present validity, that secured his interest. Logically, therefore, his sense of being "transferred" was only a stage in the task of using the historical examples to confront the problems of the contemporary world.

Machiavelli therefore anticipates Marx's comments about the "heroes . . . of the old French Revolution" who "performed the task of their time in Roman costume and with Roman phrases." He was, however, unsuccessful in his attempt to reform Florentine policies; by contrast (and in Marx's view) the French revolutionaries succeeded in "the task of unchaining and setting up modern bourgeois society" (*EB*, 11). Yet this reference to the revolutionary period brings into focus once again the distinction that has already been made in the course of this study: between the exemplary, monumental approach of neoclassicism (David's *Socrates*) and the divided, not to say incoherent, discourse of the new painting of the French Restoration (Coupin's *Sully*). It was a misfortune for France that (again in Marx's terms) "its real military leaders sat behind the office desks, and the hog-headed Louis XVIII was its political chief" (*EB*, 11). But from the point of view of historical representation, it was not simply that contemporary politics insisted on supplying unheroic figures: the entire view of the past, as it amplified and deepened throughout the Romantic period, offered innumerable new points of identification, which could not possibly be exhausted by the stale repertoire of the Bourbon Restoration.

Yet it is precisely in the pluralism of the Restoration period that we begin to find markers for the idea of "living the past." Marx wrote his *Eighteenth Brumaire* in order to analyze how it was that the adventurer Louis Napoleon had persuaded the French people to entrust him with reviving the Empire of his uncle, the first Napoleon, after 1848; in Marx's words, it was a question of showing how "the *class struggle* in France created circumstances and relationships that made it possible for a grotesque mediocrity to play a hero's part" (*EB*, 6). Our purpose here is to examine just one strand in the historical propaganda used by the Bourbon dynasty, whose elder and younger branches reigned in France from the final expulsion of Napoleon in 1815 until the 1848 Revolution. This will be shown to be one of the components in the idea of "living the past."

In 1824, the French sculptor François-Joseph Bosio showed at the Salon his life-sized statue of *Henri IV as a Child*, a work originally commissioned by the Ministry of the Interior for the French city of Pau, Henri IV's birthplace. Bosio was originally a native of Monaco, who had volunteered for the French revolutionary armies and later journeyed to Italy, where he worked in the studio of the foremost neoclassical sculptor of the day, Antonio Canova. On his return to France, around 1807, he received several official commissions, including one for a massive lead statue of Napoleon, destined for the Arc de Triomphe of the Carousel, which was never erected. His conversion to the service of the new dynasty was, however, rapid, since he showed a bust of Louis XVIII in the Salon of 1814. In 1822 he received the honorary appointment of "Premier sculpteur du Roi."

Bosio's statue of Henri IV was an instant success. While the marble version went to Pau as arranged (and a version in bronze as shown here has ended up in the château), a special silver version was ordered for the aging Louis XVIII, who installed it in his bed-

19. The silver version was installed in the King's bedroom: Bosio, *Henri IV as a Child* (1824).

room. Clearly, the slight but pugnacious boy, who grasps the pommel of his sword and looks fixedly into the distance, appealed to this latter-day head of the Bourbon family. He derives little, it would seem, from the cool classicism of Bosio's master, Canova, suggesting instead a distant kinship with the youthful Davids of the Renaissance master, Donatello. But his costume is not biblical; his tight jerkin, slashed breeches, and artfully wrinkled hose are redolent of the late sixteenth century. It is not clear if Bosio used a precise model for his features. There is, however, a contemporary painting reputed to be of the young prince, which was at this time in the collection of the Orléans family and suits Bosio's characterization quite closely.[4]

Images of Henri IV had almost immediately greeted the return of the Bourbons in 1814. In that very year, Abraham Constantin decorated a large Sèvres vase with a portrait of the founder of the dynasty, based on an original by Pourbus. Quick thinking had been necessary to compliment the new regime with this flattering work, as the vase was destined to bear the image of the Empress Marie-Louise. Two further Sèvres vases, which like that of Constantin are kept in the Château de Pau, testify to the growing concern with public representations of Henri IV that marked the early years of the Restoration; painted by Jean-Charles Develly, these objects record the removal of an original statue of the king on 18 August 1818 and its inauguration in a new position of honor by the Pont-Neuf on 25 August 1818.[5]

There are indeed innumerable instances of the prominence of Henri IV in the iconography of this period. They range from medals struck to commemorate his connection with the Bourbons of the Restoration to the applied arts, sculpture, and, of course, painting. And indeed it could be argued that Henri IV was a national figure of such great importance that he had never been far from the center of attention when French artists and writers turned, in the course of the eighteenth century, to the investigation of national and historical themes. In the early days of the Empire, the young Prosper de Barante, taking time off from his training in the imperial civil service to write a series of drama criticisms, acclaimed the performance of the great classical actor Talma in the first production of Legouvé's play *La Mort de Henri IV*.[6] Yet this reference to the play, which Stendhal was later to brand as "antiromantic,"[7] only serves to accentuate the originality of Bosio's sculpture. Granted that Henri IV's assassination had been thought an appropriate theme for tragedy—

granted that the Restoration had brought forth a spate of images recording the Bourbons' progenitor with different degrees of timeliness—who ever thought of presenting the great warrior and architect of national unity as a child?

In fact, Bosio's sculpture can be said to have fitted a double bill. It is surely germane to its effect to point out that the Bourbon dynasty, newly returned to France but grown old and decrepit in their years of exile, had at first possessed no young male heir to assure the succession. Of the two brothers of the guillotined Louis XVI who came back in 1814, the elder—crowned Louis XVIII—was childless, while his brother—who was to reign as Charles X between 1824 and 1830—had a son but no male grandchild. After the assassination of this son, the Duc de Berry, in 1820, his wife gave birth in 1820 to the "enfant de miracle," who became the future head of the elder branch of the Bourbons under the title of Duc de Bordeaux. Surely Bosio's timely sculpture, which celebrates the vigorous and healthy childhood of the founder of the family, can be viewed as a wager placed upon the future of the Bourbons, and much more emphatically so than the many images of Henri IV in his prime or at the moment of his fateful death? It takes attention away from Marx's "hog-headed" Louis XVIII and predicts that the past can return again, not in the form of gout-ridden princes recovering from decades of exile but in the much more palatable spectacle of an alert and capable youth whose blood still flows through the veins of his progeny.

But if we accept this as the ideological message of Bosio's work, we have to admit that it is an unstable one. The historical staging of the contrast between youth and age brings equivocal results. Just as in the case of Coupin's *Sully*, there is in the first place an uncertainty as to whether the work offers itself to be read from a monumental or an antiquarian point of view. Should we focus on the golden heart of Henri IV as an object of reverence and emulation, or should we be distracted by the fashionable period dress of the young Prince de Henrichemont? The ambivalence is no less great with Bosio's Henri IV. Does the statue inspire sentiments favorable to the persistence of the Bourbon dynasty, or does the princely child simply come across as a charming representative of a historical period? From the way that the motif of Henri IV develops in the art of the Restoration, we can say that the second alternative may be more appropriate, or at least that the two types of reading are inextricably intertwined.

The antiquarian image of the young Bourbon is already anticipated in a work like Ingres's *Don Pedro de Tolède baisant l'epée de
Henri IV* (1819, Musée national du Château de Pau). The future
King of France is here depicted at a more advanced age than in
Bosio's work; he is no doubt already King of Navarre, a title to
which he succeeded at the age of nineteen. But Ingres has been at
pains to accentuate the formal and psychological contrast between
the finely dressed, oddly diffident young man and the robust, dark-
cloaked Spaniard who kneels to kiss his sword with a flourish. Thus
the dramatic interest of the little scene lies in a kind of rhetorical
reversal of the expected relationship: the king is slender, even a
little effete, but he commands the allegiance of the florid grandee.

Ingres's painting reflects the antiquarian, slightly precious conventions of the "style troubadour," in which costume details are
rendered with minute attention; it also incorporates the edge of a
spectacular portico, with supporting caryatids, on the extreme left.
But the device of using the youth of Henri IV to endorse a fresh
and vivid image of a period milieu survives the decline of the "style
troubadour" and culminates in one of the largest and most opulently
colored paintings of the entire Restoration: Eugène-Marie-François
Devéria's *Naissance de Henri IV* (1827, Musée du Louvre). In this
work, described as "the manifesto of young Romantic painting,"[8]
the whole of the court of Navarre is arranged like a great floral
bouquet around its center, which is the tiny body of the infant
prince. An early sketch for the composition (Musée Fabre, Montpel-
lier) demonstrates this remarkable vitality of form and coloring,
while the finished version shows that Devéria has learned from
Veronese in particular to use the variegated effects of period costume for an integrated aesthetic effect. By this stage in the Restoration, the lingering ideological aspects of the cult of Henri IV must
have persisted only in an attenuated form, and Devéria's exercise
in historical representation could be seen in the same terms as that
other outstanding success of the 1827 Salon: Delacroix's *Sardanapalus*. On the level of pure painting, the death scene of the sadistic
Assyrian monarch and the birth of the first of the Bourbon dynasty
offered much common ground.

Yet I have no intention of implying that, in this case, the passage
from "troubadour" minuteness to the broad brushes of the Romantic school led to a jettisoning of historical reference in favor of ab-
stract aesthetic effect. What I wish to suggest is that historical
representation distanced itself, by an inevitable development of its

20. The King surprised on his knees: Richard Parkes Bonington, *Henry IV and the Spanish Ambassador* (1827).

intrinsic aims and properties, from the ideological support of the Bourbon regime. But this did not mean an abandonment of history; it simply meant the relinquishment of the myth that the restored Bourbons could live again through visual symbols like the young Henri IV. Here it is worth referring once again to the work of Bonington, who admittedly, as an Englishman, has less reason to be sensitive to the requirements of French politics. Bonington was sufficiently impressed by Devéria's *Henri IV* to make a copy of it in 1827, and in the same year he completed the delightful small oil *Henri IV and the Spanish Ambassador* (Wallace Collection, London). In this work, Henri IV is not a child, but he is playing with his children, one of whom clambers onto his back as the disconcerted ambassador enters through curtains to the right.

Bonington is making a serious historical point in this painting, as well as creating a charming rhetorical effect. The king who has been endowed with all the gravity of hindsight is reclaimed for our imagination by this display of surprising humanity and kindliness. In a further related painting dating from the next year, *Henri III and the English Ambassador* (1828, Wallace Collection, London), Bonington uses the contemporary memoirs of Don Juan of Austria to create a lively impression of a king who was a Valois, not a Bourbon, and in all events the very opposite of a warrior king. The rather vapid-looking young king is shown with a pet monkey and a brilliant assortment of parrots, holding a fan of peacock's feathers in his drooping white hand. Yet the close antiquarian study, evident from the details of furniture and costume in both this and the previous painting, is not belied by this concern to display the unexpected and therefore memorable scene. Quite the opposite, the two aspects work together within the compass of Bonington's pictorial style.

Bonington's most curious tribute to the cult of Henri IV was, however, a sketch that was destined for a history painting never to be completed. *Henri IV's Bedchamber at the Château de La Roche-Guyon* (c. 1825, Richard Feigen, New York) derives from the artist's visit to the place where the king retired after the Battle of Ivry in 1590. During the Restoration, the château was the property of the Duc de Rohan-Chabot, who "hosted frequent 'medieval' receptions in the grounds" and was altogether willing to show visitors the spectacular "king's bed" that was thought to date from the time of Henri IV's tenancy. Bonington has represented the great bed, with its fine garnet velour curtains, and he has also shown a period armchair, drawn up at the foot of the bed, as the light floods in from an adjacent window. But there is no Henri IV present. Or rather, since the figure of the king is not included, the imagination is left to exercise itself on the multiple possibilities of this strategic absence, Patrick Noon speculates: "It is impossible . . . to ignore the monumental presence of the royal bed. An extraordinary piece of furniture in its own right, the bed, with its picturesque visual attributes and its association with the amorous adventures of this monarch, alone offered a compelling pretext for the choice of subject. Its patriarchal symbolism would also have held a special meaning for a generation intent on demonstrating the legitimacy of Henri IV's lineage" (Noon, 166–67).

Here is a plausible statement of some of the historical connotations that would have attached to Bonington's eloquently empty armchair. Indeed, it is quite right to question (as Noon does) the retrospective analysis that determines that Bonington, being a "pure painter," delighted in historical subject matter because he was ultimately unconcerned with any form of content. Where Léon Rosenthal asserts, with some pride, that "nothing matches the insignificance of his historical pictures" (Noon, 63), he is imposing a present-day judgment on a sensibility that was alert to a whole range of types of significance. The fact that Bonington in no way endorsed the recuperation of Henri IV by the restored Bourbon dynasty does not imply that he was not deeply versed in the historical and antiquarian culture of his period. On the contrary, his works indicate an exceptional awareness of the new domains opened up to the creative imagination by historical research, coupled always with a shrewd artistic sense of the plastic and rhetorical means necessary for him to contribute, in his own medium, to the developing discourse.

It may appear artificial to proffer the statue of the young Henri IV as evidence of the desire of the elder branch of the Bourbon dynasty to "live the past," especially when I am also interested in stressing the skill of artists like Devéria and Bonington at converting the motif to their own purposes. Yet the sequel to this infatuation with the image of Henri IV is a surprising one. The younger branch of the Bourbon family, which came to the throne after the July Revolution of 1830 in the person of Louis-Philippe, was also of course descended from Henri IV and, having driven the elder branch into exile, was perhaps more in need of historical legitimation. Certainly, no contemporary European monarch was more preoccupied with the celebration of the national past than Louis-Philippe. His decision to set up the "Musée historique" at Versailles in 1833 involved an undertaking unprecedented in its scale, dedicated to "all the glories of France." As Marie-Claude Chaudonneret has indicated, the seeds for this pioneering expression of national "heritage" were sown at an earlier stage in the Bourbon Restoration, when the project of the Musée Charles X was developed for the redecoration of the Louvre. But nothing in these earlier plans equaled the grandiose conception of the Galerie des batailles at Versailles, which traced the construction of nationhood from the Frankish king Clovis to the recent triumphs of Napoleon and Louis-Philippe himself.[9]

What concerns us here, however, is a more intimate, yet no less fascinating, use of the past, which extended to an ultimate degree the identification of the Bourbon family with the figure of Henri IV. The Château de Pau, birthplace of the monarch who had succeeded in 1572 to the tiny kingdom of Navarre and in 1589 to the throne of France, was a splendidly sited fortress overlooking the Pyrenees, which until the sixteenth century played very little part in the history of France. As the capital of the vicomté of Béarn, Pau itself merged into the neighboring county of Foix in the thirteenth century. Eventually, when the counts of Foix became kings of Navarre in the fifteenth century, the old feudal château became one of their principal seats. Yet Henri IV's translation onto the national scale meant that neither he nor his Bourbon successors had much time to spare for the cradle of their family. The Château de Pau slumbered throughout the next two centuries and by the end of the Revolution was in a seriously ruined state. It was this building that Louis-Philippe determined to restore as a residence for himself and his family. Unlike the elder branch of the Bourbons, the Orléans branch did not want for young and vigorous male heirs, who would gain in prestige and authority by being identified with the birthplace of Henri IV.

Louis-Philippe's restoration of the Château de Pau, which commenced in 1838, involved major architectural changes that were supervised by the architects Lefranc and Paul Abbadie (the latter being also responsible for important works of church renovation carried out at the time, such as those at the cathedral of Saint-Front at Périgueux). A new "Louis-Philippe tower" was erected to create a balanced effect for the exterior, and a chapel, built in the place of a former entry, was dedicated in the presence of one of the Orléans sons, the Duc de Montpensier, in 1843. But what was most remarkable and innovative was the furnishing of the main state rooms. To a great extent, the furniture in the great reception salons and the state bedrooms was specially designed for them; it represented a coherent decorative plan that was neither contemporary (in the sense of using currently fashionable styles) nor traditional (in the sense of using original seventeenth-century pieces) but historicist in character. As it is usual to explain, the inspiration behind the new decor was to be found specifically in the paintings of the "style troubadour."

The restoration and furnishing of the Château de Pau forms a specially significant episode, for our purposes, since it demonstrates a clear point about the working of the historical imagination in this phase of its development. Louis-Philippe certainly had no concept of returning the building to the state in which it had been at the time of Henri IV's birth. Indeed, any concept of an authentic reminiscence of his presence at Pau seems to have been ruled out. It is in more recent years that the newly founded museum has set itself the task of accumulating objects with a proven connection to Henri IV: namely, his turtle-shell cradle, two forks, and a tric-trac board bearing his monogram. Louis-Philippe, not averse to improving the external silhouette of the building, also wished for repleteness and totality in the refurbished interior rather than the punctual presence of individual authentic items. Consequently, he passed by way of the totalizing matrix of a style, the "style troubadour." Everything would have the seamless effect of an achieved representation, as in the historical paintings of Fleury Richard, Pierre-Henri Revoil, and Ingres (in his troubadour phase).

This aim could not, of course, be achieved without a certain amount of trickery. In the *Chambre de Jeanne d'Albret*, named after Henri IV's mother, there is a heavily ornamented wooden bed, inscribed with the date 1562 and bearing in a cartouche the motif of the cow, which is the emblem of Béarn. Despite the striking effect of this magnificent piece of furniture, which is adorned with carvings on biblical and symbolic themes, a close inspection has ascertained that it is a composite piece, which incorporates several separate items from the sixteenth century. The same goes for the seemingly medieval oak coffers in the same room, which have been carefully designed to set off the period fragments in a new construction. For the larger and more public rooms, however, Louis-Philippe had to rely on decorators who painted with a broader brush. The previous throne room of the kings of Navarre, which had also been the place of Henri IV's baptism in 1554, was divided into two magnificent adjoining salons, unified visually by a series of gilt-bronze chandeliers in "troubadour" style and a set of oak armchairs designed by Jeanselme. Of all these sumptuously carved chairs, there is just one that stands out in being even more finely oramented than its peers. Where the others bear blank medallions on their backs, this individual one is enhanced with a proud "H" for Henri.

Even to the specifying of an individual "throne" in memory of the *genius loci*, the interior decoration of the Château de Pau represented in concrete terms the claim of the Orléans family to live in the spirit of their ancestor. It is not surprising that the monarch who succeeded Louis-Philippe found it politic to continue the identification. Napoleon III, nephew of the great Napoleon, had not the slightest claim to be considered a descendant of Henri IV. But his wife was a Spanish countess, and Pau was conveniently close to the fashionable watering place of Biarritz. Consequently, the imperial family spent many holidays at the Château de Pau, and Napoleon himself took in hand the further embellishment of the building, which inevitably comprised the erection of a Napoleon III tower on the opposite side to Louis-Philippe's addition. Shortly after Napoleon's exile in 1870, the process that had sought to turn Pau into a historical backdrop for the legitimation of France's post revolutionary monarchs came to a close. When one of the presidents of the Third Republic made an official addition to the collection of the château, he chose, understandably, to offer nothing more controversial than a large Chinese vase. But the decision of the French state to open a Musée national at Pau in 1927 inevitably involved despatching to the château a host of objects relating to Henri IV, from the tric-trac board to the creations of the "style troubadour" on which the concept of Louis-Philippe's furnishing was based. As it exists today, the Château de Pau is a remarkable palimpsest, where differing modes and codes of historical representation exist, as if in archaeological layers. France's chequered history, from the time of the Revolution onwards, is offered for analysis in terms of the successive investments of its rulers in the national myth of Henri IV. Meanwhile, *Henri IV enfant*, in Bosio's bronze version, gazes across at the empty armchair bearing his monogram.

◆

The historical museum of the present day is an incoherent, or at least an ironic, discourse. In its determination to historicize everything within its compass, it disavows the fact that historicism was itself the production of a particular moment in history and that the sense of the past will inevitably express itself through representation. Indeed, the main purpose of this study is to stress the complexity of historical representation and to show how it depends on the intermeshing of different discursive elements. If the Château de Pau is designed to be a place where the younger Bourbons can live historically, it can fulfill this role only through mobilizing the appropriate symbols and communicating them in a vivid and comprehensible way. Yet this process is itself subject to a kind of inevitable entropy: it was not only the instability of French institutions in the nineteenth century that forced successive sovereigns out of their carefully established historical roles but the instability of the whole notion of historical mimetism, when carried to these extremes. Within a few years after the fall of Napoleon III, the whole vast undertaking of the restored interior was misunderstood, or at any rate rejected, with the effect that the furniture was put into storage, and only reemerged after World War II. It had ceased to be *discours* and could appear only as *histoire* the second time round.

Yet it can be argued that the pioneers of Romantic historical-mind-edness already recognized this fact, and that irony—Vico's "double vision," which sees things from a reserved as well as an empathetic stance—was integral to their achievements. Insofar as the representation of the past was a discourse, implying a subject communicating to other subjects, it took into account the other side of the illusion; that is to say, it maintained a critical distance from even the most accomplished re-creative feats. One of the most convincing proofs of this hypothesis can be found in the account of Alexandre du Sommerard's Musée de Cluny by Madame de Saint-Surin, which appeared in 1835, not long after the newly installed collection had been made available to the public. Du Sommerard can truly be seen as one of the most influential practitioners in "staging the past": his decision to mass together historical objects of everyday use in the "period" rooms of the old townhouse of the Abbots of Cluny made possible a concrete experience of the past that was perhaps unprecedented in its intensity.[10] Yet it is interesting to observe that Madame de Saint-Surin is concerned precisely to stress the discursive element: the museum is not a replica of the past but a kind of dialogue between past and present, a conversation between youth and age:

> Gothic France here makes an alliance with the new France; all the ages are present. It seemed to us that these so different epochs would lend each other a mutual support, and that the frozen debris of past centuries would be reanimated by the whirlwind of our bustling actuality. In this way, across these grand images of what exists no longer, beside these slim caryatids which support the bed of the brave and gallant François I, we were pleased to hear the sweet and fresh voice of a young elegant woman, who, with her light remark, had just removed the wrinkles from the meditative forehead of a grave person who was deeply absorbed in thinking of the middle ages at the sight of the ebony panels, artistically chiseled, of a gothic cabinet. The world thrives on contrasts.[11]

Madame de Saint-Surin would presumably have disapproved of Louis-Philippe's decision to furnish the Château de Pau in the "style troubadour," since she deplored the tendency of "modern artists" to imitate and reproduce the "gothic furniture" featured in Du Sommerard's collection: it was "as if our society had given up the privilege of invention" (Saint-Surin, 10). But her most interesting remarks are reserved for two installations in the Musée de Cluny that particularly concern us, since they both imply the illusion of lifelike presence in the museum: "living the past." It is significant that one of these attracts her wholehearted admiration and the other her equally strong disapproval. The first reaction is reserved for the most celebrated of Du Sommerard's rooms:

> Lifting up the tapestries across the doorways, we pass into the Room of François I. His bed is there, with elegant caryatids supporting the roof; his armour is laid out on the counterpane; you would think it was the hero resting! Two knights standing at the foot of the bed, with lance in hand and lowered visor, seem to stand guard still over their master. At the sight of these pictorial episodes, the imagination is struck and tempted to take the marvel for reality. (Saint-Surin, 24)

The print of the *Chambre dite de François Ier*, published in Du Sommerard's *Les Arts au moyen âge* (1838–46), shows the bed in which the king was reputed to have slept in recognizably the same condition as Madame de Saint-Surin describes it, though the custom of arranging the royal armor on the bed, like evening clothes, seems to have been discontinued. The meticulous visitor is also enthusiastic about the presence of the chess set of rock crystal, "precisely the same . . . as was sent to Saint Louis by the prince of the Assassins," which is arranged on a board in the window embrasure: "two knights seated in face of one another are getting ready to move the first pawns; and certainly with less imagination than Hoffmann had when he wrote his fantastic tales, it appears as if you are present at this game" (Saint-Surin, 28).

The mention of the German writer E.T.A. Hoffmann is interesting, since it shows that Madame de Saint-Surin measures her level of credulity by the same standards as the "fantastic" fiction of the day. Yet even she is unwilling to connive at what she regards as a blatant attempt by Du Sommerard to milk the emotions of his public (the cause of offense is once again quite visible in the contemporary print):

> Most of the visitors repaired to the chapel where you can see, in the forms appropriate to the Middle Ages, all the

21. The knights stand guard over their master: *Vue de la Chambre dite de François Ier*, from *Les Arts au moyen âge* (1838–46).

furnishings suitable for a place of prayer. One thing alone seemed to us to contrast with the gravity of the place: this is a statue clothed in priestly robes which is standing before the lectern.

When you are on the point of penetrating into the oratory of the widow of Louis XII, you expect to find there a mysterious solitude; and the appearance of this canon of stone, in ceremonial costume, standing, motionless, with a face either pale or illuminated (we could not vouch for the colour of his complexion, for we shut our eyes), becomes for some a subject of surprise; whilst the others . . . can only see the bizarre side of this phantom. (Saint-Surin, 39)

What was Du Sommerard intent on achieving when he slipped this incongruous ''chanoine de pierre'' into the chapel of the Musée de Cluny? It would, on one level, be perfectly fair to see his installation as the ancestor of the myriad attempts to ''bring the past to life'' that have accompanied the development of the tourist trade in postwar

22. Surprised by a canon in stone: *Chapel, Hôtel de Cluny,* from *Les Arts au moyen âge* (1838–46).

Europe and America. The rhetoric of historical resurrection has changed little over the years. Thus *The Canterbury Tales*, permanently installed in the deconsecrated church of Saint Margaret's in Canterbury, proclaims in its publicity: "At The Canterbury Tales you can step back in time to the 14th century. Experience and enjoy the sights, sounds and even the smells of the period."[12] In a not dissimilar way, Emile Deschamps enthused about the effect of the Musée de Cluny in 1834: "you walk in the midst of a vanished civilisation; you are as if enveloped by the good old chivalric times."[13] In both cases, the emphasis is on an "enveloping" experience, not confined to visual perception alone; and while Cluny had its "chanoine de pierre" and its chess-playing suits of armor, Canterbury peoples its converted church with life-size replicas of the different characters in Chaucer's rumbustious saga of the medieval world.

Yet there is a crucial difference. In the first place, we should note the comparative discretion of Du Sommerard's evocations. Like the outsize suit of armor that stands over Scott as he works in his study, the variously disposed knights of the *Chambre dite de François Ier* are not replicas, but imaginative intimations of a human presence. It is Madame de Saint-Surin who herself makes the connection: "you would think it was the hero resting!" She may well conclude that in the chapel Du Sommerard has gone a stage too far: he has misjudged the psychological disposition of the visitors to the chapel and invaded the "mysterious solitude" that they have the right to expect. Despite this criticism, we can have no doubt that Madame de Saint-Surin respects the basis of Du Sommerard's medieval fabulation: as the reference to Hoffmann implies, it can be found in the developing codes of Romantic literature, where the concept of the "fantastic" allows precisely this kind of exquisite equivocation between the real and the unreal.[14] The historical re-creations of our own time, by contrast, take as their model an infinitely more complex technological apparatus for reproducing reality as an effect. As Umberto Eco remarks, with reference to the later Romantics: "What would Ruskin, Morris and the pre-Raphaelites have said if they had been told that the rediscovery of the Middle Ages would be the work of the twentieth-century mass media?"[15]

Yet it is not only a question of degree. Du Sommerard's Musée de Cluny was different from the contemporary theme park not merely because he lacked appropriate technology to simulate "the smells of the period" but also because his role in the discourse of the museum was of paramount importance. Emile Deschamps concludes the passage quoted earlier by writing: "and the cordial presence of the master rounds off the illusion." We may indeed suppose that Du Sommerard was present, whenever possible, to do the honors of his collection: to recount the history of individual items like the rock-crystal chess set and to offer a guiding thread through rooms crammed with so many unfamiliar historical objects. More than this, we can confidently assert that the Musée de Cluny was universally perceived as Du Sommerard's collection. Even when Madame de Saint-Surin lets her pen wander in a personal re-creation of her visit, she is never in any doubt that it is Du Sommerard who has devised the whole experience. "We are glad to offer our homage," she writes, "to the enlightened man who brings together and causes to be restored so many rarities, industrial and artistic masterpieces deriving from our forefathers, at the period of the Renaissance" (Saint-Surin, vi).

The point may seem obvious. But it is crucial to the argument of this study. For what is at stake, once again, is the difference between *histoire* and *discours*. The contemporary historical spectacle is all too often alienated from the subject of discourse in its overriding pursuit of intense, illusionistic effects. It aims, paradoxically, to represent the past as past, *wie es eigentlich gewesen*, but at the same time to fill the senses with immediate, "hyperreal" stimuli. Du Sommerard understood that a historical collection required at the same time a replete, responsive environment (such as the Hôtel de Cluny) and a voice to assume the duty of mediating between past and present. The Bourbon kings who reigned throughout the period in which he built up, who installed and popularized his collection, may have set great store by the idea of "living the past." Their dynastic concerns led them to represent in material form the historical identification with Henri IV that was vital to their survival. Yet Du Sommerard trusted to the more modest objective of "bringing the past to life." Compared with the expensive commissions for the Château de Pau, his installations at the Hôtel de Cluny offered particularized and closely focused objects whose discursive articulation he was able to achieve in the speech of his commentary and the prose of his catalogue. By contrast with the ideologically overdetermined figure of Henri IV, Du Sommerard could provide an open invitation to imagine the presence of François I, through the metonymic suggestion of the objects that had brushed against him.

◆

This chapter began with a reference to the moving letter Machiavelli wrote from his Tuscan farm to describe how he was "transferred" into the company of the classical historians and how he took off his everyday clothes and put on "panni reali e curiali" to make himself worthy of the occasion. It also alluded to a present-day photograph of men wearing the uniforms of the American Civil War and preparing to reenact one of its battles. What I have been describing in the context of the French Restoration is the different stages through which the idea of "living the past" became manifest, not as a stratagem for addressing the political issues of the present (as in Machiavelli's case) but as an uneasy blend of ideological and aesthetic components. The Bourbon cult of Henri IV demonstrates the problematic nature of this combination, just as the achievement of Alexandre du Sommerard suggests a more powerful and effective means of articulating a relationship to the past. Yet if Du Sommerard dressed his "chanoine en pierre" in priestly costume, he did not dress up himself. He was content to be a shifter between the represented world and the world of his fashionable Parisian visitors, who were allowed to make their own "light remarks," like the "elegant young woman" mentioned by Madame de Saint-Surin.

A more intensive stage of historical mimetism had to wait, no doubt, for the more and more extensive diffusion of the historical materials that Du Sommerard had begun to popularize and for a more and more conclusive disconnection between the use of history for ideological purposes and its potentiality as a domain of pure representation. Francis Haskell refers to the unusually intense research into the past conducted by a close friend of Hippolyte Taine, the journalist and collector Emile-Marcelin-Isidore Planat. Taine first met Planat in 1846, almost at the end of the July Monarchy: his guiding passion was for the collection of historical engravings, of which "he eventually accumulated some three hundred thousand" (Haskell, 347). But Planat's avid collecting was simply a means of entering, through empathy and knowledge, the different historical periods conveyed by his sources. As Taine relates, "he would speak as if he had lived in those times . . . he had an entry into five or six worlds, each as complete as our own. Without any conscious effort of the will he would enter them . . . He felt at home and relaxed—more relaxed than in our own world" (quoted in Haskell,

348). Taine himself felt extremely ambivalent about this habit of entering into the different historical periods through the medium of the visual arts, which he conceived to be a falsification of the true nature of historical development. But he was evidently impressed by the sheer interest of the phenomenon, acknowledging Planat to have been a "true historian." It was, indeed, a cultural and psychological event of some significance that the past should be so successfully colonized by the plastic power of the individual imagination; and this "desire for history" had no obvious ideological justification, except insofar as Planat preferred to set aside the contemporary world in favor of the rich vicarious experience of the preceding centuries.

Of Planat's time-traveling we have, however, only the indirect record provided by the testimony of Taine. For an illustration of the fascinating, though ambiguous, results of an even more ambitious exercise, which has left its traces behind, we have only to turn to the life and work of the French novelist Pierre Loti. This indefatigable collector and constructor, born under the name of Julien Viaud on 14 January 1850, transformed his modest family home in the French port of Rochefort-sur-Mer into a rich assemblage of historical and exotic interiors. Half a century before, at the height of the Romantic period, Sir Walter Scott had undertaken the building of Abbotsford, which was both a fantastic projection of an image of medieval baronial life and a strategy for recovering his family's rightful place on the banks of the Tweed (see Bann 1984, 93–111). Loti's birthplace, which he bought from his mother in 1871 and aggrandized through the purchase of the neighboring house in 1895, was simply one unit in a long, straight street of decorous white stone buildings. Even today, since the urban texture of the town has remained remarkably homogeneous, it is difficult to locate the "maison de Pierre Loti" along the receding perspective of the street that bears his name. But behind the facade the interior explodes into a series of spectacular individual spaces, each complete in its own terms and issuing virtually without transition onto its neighbour.

These spaces that Loti created over the course of almost twenty years comprised oriental as well as historical re-creations. Indeed, it is one of the distinctive features of Loti's imaginative world that projections into the spatial "other" of the Near and Far East should be treated pari passu with projections into the temporal "other" of European history. He began his work on the house in 1886, on his return from a voyage to Nagasaki, when he set up a "Japanese pagoda" close to the main entrance. This installation (now dismounted) was a very modest undertaking by comparison with his next enterprise in 1887, which was the creation of a medieval room, or "Salle gothique," on the second floor of the building, looking away from the street. For this interior, Loti brought together a large number of heterogenous pieces of woodwork and stonework, some of them of local provenance and others from further afield, and combined them into a unified effect that is truly startling in its intensity. This illusion of authenticity was achieved through clever adaptation of some of the major medieval fragments to the aesthetic and structural requirements of the existing building. For example, Loti has installed a range of fine *flamboyant* Gothic windows taken from a demolished local church, but he has reversed them, so that the deep moldings are visible from the inside, and the stonework fits flush with the eighteenth-century facade on the outside.

Abbotsford, set in its splendid position on the river bank, offered landscape views over a wide area and no inconvenient prospects of the modern world. Loti had to content himself instead with turning the emphasis of the long, narrow townhouse away from the street, opening up the interiors into self-enclosed, stylistically unified spaces. But in the case of the "Salle gothique," he has anticipated the likelihood that one of his visitors would peer out of the medieval windows in order to see if the illusion might be shattered by the sight of lowly modern domestic arrangements. The adjacent building (formerly the property of his maternal grandfather and bought back by Loti) exhibits a small Gothic window and a suitably grotesque gargoyle: even the view is controlled in such a way as to suggest that the medieval world contains (and is contained by) the Gothic chamber.

The photographs Loti had taken to celebrate the completion of this historical room are both curious and revealing. Scott was customarily painted in two guises, which were liable to become confused. On the one hand, he was the professional writer in his study, on the other, the country gentleman surrounded by his dogs or profiled against the Scottish scenery. Loti has taken advantage of the development of photography to show us the extraordinarily elaborate detail of the neomedieval milieu: its wooden surfaces gleam, and we can almost sense the textures of its magnificent hangings. He has also installed himself strategically in the midst of everything. Defiantly modern in his clothing, and leaning back at an unnatural angle that may have been forced upon him by the

23. The invitation to enter the past: Pierre Loti in his *Salle gothique* (c. 1887).

exposure time, Loti subjectively takes charge of the historical scene. It is not precisely as a writer that he does this—let alone as a landed proprietor—but as the possessor of an imaginative vision that has been amply materialized; one, moreover, that he invites the rest of the world to share.

The invitation should not be construed as merely metaphorical. In order to inaugurate the "Salle gothique," Pierre Loti arranged a costumed dinner for both his Parisian and his local friends, which took place on 12 April 1888 and was extensively reported in the regional press. By this stage, Loti had achieved a wide reputation for his novels, which were usually concerned with exotic and sentimental scenes and were to ensure his election to the *Académie française* in 1891. His list of invited guests thus ranged improbably from a popular writer like Juliette Adam to a man about town and *fin de siècle* dandy like Prince Bojidar Karageorgevitch; from maternal relations like his wife's brother and sister-in-law, M. and Mme. de Ferrière, to representatives of the naval establishment of Rochefort like Madame l'amirale Aurous (the commanding officers themselves, for reasons that can only be guessed at, neglected to appear in person, but were content to allow their wives to accept the invitation).[16]

This bewildering variety of invited guests was, however, much attenuated by the fact that everyone wore medieval costume and was allotted a specific role. This was to be, as the lengthy invitation card in medieval French made out, a "Dîner Louis XI," held as if it had taken place "under the reign of our good king Louis the Eleventh, around the year of grace 1470," with appropriate food and drink (Bault, 15). Thus Juliette Adam, who possessed a property near Paris at Gif-sur-Yvette, was seated at the right hand of the master of the house under the name of the Dame de Gif. Prince Karageorgevitch was reincarnated as René de Hyalange, a kind of latter-day troubadour who was given the task of finishing off the evening with "Hungarian airs" and melancholy villanelles. M. and Mme. de Ferrière, taking the names of Jean and Arlette de Nivelle, had no such performing role to play, but came dressed, like all the others, in elaborate fur-trimmed costumes, with fantastic headgear to match. The admiral's wife, as appropriate to her elevated local position, sat opposite the Dame de Gif and the tuneful prince, under the name of Berengère de Hautfort. She cannot have moved much during the long ceremony, as her long train, modeled on the court dress of fifteenth-century France, really required a trainbearer to make motion feasible.

It is easy to poke fun at this stage-managed inauguration of the "Salle gothique," or to see it as an eccentric, local event of little significance. It was, however, extensively reported. Photographic documentation of a meticulous kind enables us to see how this motley crew of late nineteenth-century aristocrats, bourgeois, and bohemians caparisoned themselves for the event. If all Rochefort could not, for obvious reasons, be seated at the table, arrangements were made for the open gallery at the end of the medieval room to be accessible to the townspeople, provided that they made some attempt at the appropriate dress, from the waist up. But the true significance of the event lay, without a doubt, in the way in which it staged the access to the medieval world of Pierre Loti himself. He ought, by rights, to have assumed the name of Louis XI himself, since his wife was credited with the role of the French queen, Charlotte de Savoie. But he understandably stopped short of this degree of historical specificity: he was to be no one in particular, by name, but simply a "seigneur of the period." In this way, he could continue to command the mise-en-scène his imagination had brought into being, shifting from his subjective role to the realized historical milieu of which he formed a part. Marie-Pascale Bault has commented with insight on the mode of participation Loti envisaged and on the significant fact that the ceremony itself was not documented in visual terms, even though its preparations were sedulously recorded:

> In Pierre Loti's mind, it is not a question of a costumed ball, or of a simple party with the past as its theme: in crossing the threshold of the room, the projection in time is supposed to be immediate, impressive and totally disorientating. What is more, this sensation of strangeness has to be maintained throughout the whole length of the evening. That is why the writer has to look after the preparation and coordination of all the different phases of the evening: the decor, the food, the menu and various interventions, undoubtedly including texts to be recited. But Loti is more than a *metteur en scène*: he is also an actor and spectator. If he takes an active part, in effect, in the dinner and the ballet which follows it, he also profits from the sketches, songs and recreational interludes. This party has to be for him a complete spectacle, conceived as a means of escape and almost a gratuitous act *(un acte presque gratuit)* to the extent that Pierre Loti will write nothing on the subject, nor even make a drawing. (Bault, 38)

When Albertine de Broglie remarked in 1825 that her generation were "the first who have understood the past" and went on to suggest that "that is largely the result of the fact that our own impressions are not strong enough," she could certainly not have predicted the degree of empathetic identification, or the corresponding disenchantment with the modern world, to which Loti's activities testify. The Romantic desire for history finds in his career a kind of ultimate fulfillment, all the more notable as it is not complicated by real dynastic or genealogical factors. Earlier in the century, Victor Hugo had invented for himself a probably spurious medieval ancestry and worked out his identification with the remote French past through a series of technically bizarre paintings and drawings (see Bann 1990, 82–99). Pierre Loti also makes play with a coat of arms, which he incorporates in the decor at Rochefort together with his wife's more authentic bearings. But it is a pure fiction, a jeu d'esprit that draws attention to its slightly ridiculous components. Loti does not appear to want to make us forget that he, at any rate, knows the difference between reality and illusion.

A further sign of Loti's curiously self-conscious disavowal of the imaginative creations he spent so much time and energy in devising can perhaps be found in the great Renaissance room installed on the ground floor of the newly acquired adjoining house in 1895. The proportions are much larger than those of the "Salle gothique," and the room incorporates not only a wooden gallery but a spectacular set of stone steps whose precipitous angle only becomes obvious to one who makes the ascent. There are fine seventeenth-century Spanish chairs to accompany the dining table and resplendent regional coffers of approximately the right period. Yet the central fireplace, which dominates the room, is a strange combination of a lower part in true Renaissance style and an upper part in Loti's beloved *flamboyant* Gothic. The Rochefort masons who worked under his supervision have carefully smoothed over the delicate transition and have installed a Spanish sixteenth-century Saint Theresa in the elaborate niche.

What is authentic here, and what is false? Loti seems to have anticipated the question by choosing for the wall hangings of the new room two fine sets of seventeenth-century tapestries (indeed, the height and proportions of the tapestries are so exactly adapted to the space that he may well have designed the whole installation with them in mind). The Oudenarde set depicts the labors of Hercules, a mythological parallel Loti may have seen as relevant to his own heroic efforts in the creation of different historical milieus. The Brussels set shows a series of episodes from the history of the "True

24. What is authentic here, and what is false?: the *Salle Renaissance* of
Pierre Loti (c. 1895).

25. The Empress solves the problem of authenticity: Brussels tapestry depicting the Empress Helena in the process of selecting the "True Cross" (seventeenth century).

Cross," whose theme of the bellicose interaction between Christian and oriental cultures may well have appealed to him. This means that turbans function iconographically in the battle between Heraclius and Chosroes, just a few yards away from the place where actual oriental turbans are to be found in his re-created Turkish mosque. But the attention is also taken by a large representation of the Empress Helena, wife of Constantine, whose legendary role was to have rediscovered the Cross upon which Christ was crucified. Standing among three apparently identical wooden crosses, she infallibly indicates which is the authentic one. This is a neat parable to have inserted in a room where every visitor must at first be mildly disconcerted at not being able to mark the dividing line between the true and the false, before recognizing that the real authenticity lies in the very gesture with which Loti designates the scene as historical.

◆

Pierre Loti's imaginative achievement at Rochefort is a fitting index of the extent to which historical consciousness had developed in the course of the nineteenth century. In Nietzsche's terms, he represents the antiquarian spirit doubled by an insistently critical turn of mind, though his criticism takes the form of a negation of the modern, Western world rather than a positive affirmation. At least we can confidently say that he is as far as possible from the "monumental" attitude; the distinctive contribution of Romanticism to historical culture can perhaps be summed up in the statement that it purged antiquarianism of the "monumental" attachments of Neoclassicism, while at the same time it permitted the ironic framing of "authenticity" to enter historical discourse as a critical element.

Yet, by these standards, Loti's achievement is also a precarious one. "Living the past" acquired an ideological tincture in the course of the nineteenth century that was to contaminate the historical culture of the twentieth. In Germany, for example, the urge to capitalize on the medieval, national past that had been revealed to Goethe through his vision of Strasbourg Cathedral took on more and more menacing forms as unification and industrialization developed apace. The spate of medieval pageantry that enlivened the public life of the Ruhrland in the years immediately prior to World War I holds a special significance in this connection, since this was a region of Germany suddenly brought into the mainstream of history by its industrial potential, after centuries of agrarian quiescence. At the Essen Jubilee of 1912 the Krupp family took the lead in organizing medieval tournaments, and contemporary photographs show Bertha and Gustav Krupp von Bohlen und Halbach in full chivalric dress accompanying the "Tournament Marshal" at the dress rehearsal. As Robert Laube queries in his informative account of these festivities, captioning a photograph in which the fully caparisoned knights thunder towards the camera, "The elite of feudalism and capitalism ride together across the lawns of the Villa Hügel—against whom?"[17]

In England, which had exhausted its appetite for revived medieval tournaments in the previous century (and was to recover it, on a more populist level, only in the contemporary period), the most poignant example of "living the past" by a man of Pierre Loti's generation must surely be that of the proprietor of Castle Drogo, known variously as "Britain's only 20th-century castle"[18] and as "the last great country house to be built from new in Britain."[19] Julius Drewe, who was born in 1856 and died in 1931, retired from business after a short but immensely profitable career helping to revolutionize the grocery trade, and devoted himself from that stage onwards to family and country life. Despite his comparatively modest origins, he conceived the idea that the Drews, or Drewes (the "e" was reintegrated for authenticity in 1910) were a family descending from a Norman baron, Drogo, or Dru, who had come over to England in the forces of William the Conqueror and given his name to the small Devon village of Drewsteignton. As he happened to have a cousin who was rector of this parish, and paid a number of visits to its spectacular site by the gorge of the River Teign, Drewe was able to nurture the idea of building his own castle in this spot, in memory of his putative ancestor. In 1910, he found the means to put his fantasy into practice by entrusting the project to the greatest British architect of the day (and certainly the only one who could have brought so ambitious a scheme to completion), Sir Edwin Lutyens.

Castle Drogo, as it stands today, is a fascinating, even bizarre, demonstration of the way in which subjective fantasy ("the desire for history") becomes grounded in the material world. Here is a building almost totally lacking in any "antiquarian" attraction. As a contemporary journalist points out: "From a distance, you can tell there is something not quite genuine about Castle Drogo. It looks rather too neat" (Barrett, 44). There is, indeed, not a hint of Riegl's "age-value" in the granite exteriors, while inside it becomes clear that Julius Drewe had little or no interest in accumulating authentic furniture but transported the contents of his former home, Wadhurst Hall, lock, stock, and barrel. As Wadhurst had been furnished according to the taste of a Spanish banker, who had been forced through bankruptcy to sell up his entire possessions, there is a medley of Spanish-style objects, mostly made in the nineteenth century but reflecting a sixteenth-century idiom. Of course, there is also a considerable amount of built-in furniture, designed by Lutyens, which achieves a particularly successful compromise between Edwardian comfort and the austerity of the unplastered granite interior.

Is Castle Drogo then essentially the creation of Lutyens, who gave it such exhaustive attention and used original devices like the inclining of the east elevation to achieve a soaring effect that accentuated the building's already considerable height? In a sense, it must undoubtedly be credited to him. But, as historical discourse, it belongs also to its initiator, Julius Drewe, who agreed that the only exterior decoration should be the heraldic lion of the Drewe family, carved above the main entrance with the family motto: "Drogo Nomen et Virtus Arma Dedit" (Drewe is the name and valour gave it arms). Julius Drewe assumes not only the authentic name but also the subjective role of summoning up this granite castle from an intensely imagined past. Lutyens conspires to achieve the vision, never failing to infiltrate critical points that bear on the authenticity of the structure. The portcullis, which hangs starkly above the entrance arch, "is no sham but a 6441b working model operated by a winch in one of the turrets" (*Drogo*, 10). It is left to the visitors to the National Trust property to make sense of all this.

Conclusion

Two popular films from the 1980s, one an English and the other an American production, demonstrate quite different ways of envisaging the subjective relationship to the past. In *Time Bandits* (1981), the young English boy Kevin (played by Craig Warnock) experiences history first of all as a kind of spectacular inruption into everyday experience. A knight in armor on horseback crashes through the wall of his bedroom and then disappears again. Impressed by this galvanizing experience, Kevin is peremptorily kidnapped by a gang of marauding dwarves ("Time Bandits") who lead him off down a rapidly receding perspective that turns out to be the entry into the past. Napoleon is the first stop—or, rather, the camp of the young general Bonaparte at a stage in the Italian campaign before the capture of Castiglione. But Kevin is taken farther and farther into the past until he reaches what appears to be the court of Agamemnon at Mycenae. There he is inclined to stay, protected by the paternal favors of the king (played by Sean Connery), except that the bandits have other plans that lead him, eventually, back to the present day.

By contrast, *Bill and Ted's Excellent Adventure* (1989) conceives time travel in a more voluntaristic way. The film is articulated around the dialogue between two goofy American teenagers (played by Keanu Reeves and Alex Winters) who journey into the past for the strictly practical task of fulfilling a class assignment. They drop in on Socrates, Genghis Khan, Joan of Arc, Billy the Kid, and Abraham Lincoln; and they contrive to bring this precious cargo of historical superstars back to the present day. Part of the film is occupied with their wide-eyed amazement at the exotic nature of the past. The other part is occupied with the experience of Socrates et al. when they are brought back to the supermarkets and hamburger stands of contemporary America, which they thoroughly appreciate despite some initial confusion. As a successful conclusion to this voyage of discovery, Bill and Ted stage their history assignment in the school auditorium before a mass audience of their peers. Since they can put on the real thing, and not merely a representation, they fully deserve to get top marks.

In this study, the main drive of the argument has been to shift the balance of historiographical study a little away from the concept indicated by *Time Bandits* and a little towards the concept implied by *Bill and Ted*. Conventional attitudes to history take for granted that historical representation—the knight in armor—is a problematic intrusion into a domain made secure by professional cognitive skills. It suffices to enter the long receding perspective of the past with a receptive eye for the evidence. What will be brought back to the present day is, at best, a conclusion drawn from the indexical traces that history has left behind (like the photographs that Kevin keeps to reassure himself that his experience of previous epochs was true, after all). But there is another approach, founded on the wider scrutiny of historical representation and on the particular urgency that was generated by the Romantic desire for the past. To treat the discursive basis of historical consciousness as it deserves, we need to evaluate the effects produced through representation: to examine the subjective stakes implied in "staging" and "living the past." This project may not get top marks, as it is a process of intricate analysis and reconstruction that by its very nature can reach no definitive conclusions. But it is perhaps a necessary corrective to the positivity that still dogs our historical awareness at many levels.

It may be asked at this point: what does the study of historical representation in the context of the Romantic movement teach us in general terms, as opposed to the specific insights that can be obtained from looking at each individual case? It is not easy to sum up the results of this investigation in the form of a conventional intellectual history. By using visual examples of widely differing types, I have endeavored to show that such representations of the past are not merely to be taken as symptoms (though they certainly can be analyzed as such) but as concrete embodiments of the different subjective positions and the diverse communicative aims that are implied in historical discourse. The image does not simply record a usage. It has a generative force or, as Louis Marin would put it, a "power."[1] It is historical culture in the making as well as the record of cognitive skills already acquired. We may be willing to accept, up to a point, the thesis that Michelet "invented" the Renaissance (see Haskell, 273–77). But to look at Paul Delaroche's *Childhood of Pico de la Mirandola* (1842) is to do more than track a concept as it begins to figure in the map of historical consciousness. It is to witness the precise moves that were necessary, through the medium of representation, for the new idea to be born.[2]

The final justification for this approach remains within the framework laid down twenty years ago in Hayden White's *Metahistory*. The *"history* of historical consciousness in nineteenth-century Europe" can also contribute to "current discussion of the *problem of historical knowledge"* (White 1973, 1). Indeed it is difficult to see how debates about historical knowledge could ever have been carried on without this dimension of historical reference. For the 1990s, such debates have tended to assume an alienated form, turning around such fetishized notions as "heritage" and "conservation," as if these were independent areas of knowledge and practice that could be divorced from the wider study of historical-mindedness. Although this study has rarely touched on these contemporary issues in an explicit way, it has always kept them surreptitiously in mind. In this domain, as in so many others, writing the history of the past is the most productive (and perhaps the only) way of writing the history of the present.

Chronology

1764   Johann Winckelmann, *History of Ancient Art*.

1769   Bryan Faussett begins work on his pavilion.

1772   Johann-Wolfgang von Goethe, *On German Architecture*.

1787   Jacques-Louis David, *Death of Socrates*.

1789   Outbreak of French Revolution.

1790   Edmund Burke, *Reflections on French Revolution*.

1793   Execution of Louis XVI.

1794   Terror and fall of Robespierre.

1795   Alexandre Lenoir begins Musée des monuments français.

1796   Napoleon Bonaparte invades Italy.

1798   William Wordsworth, *Lyrical Ballads*.

1800   Foundation of Consulate in France.

1802   Peace of Amiens between Britain and France. François-René de Châteaubriand, *Génie du Christianisme*.

1804   Napoleon crowned in Notre-Dame.

1805   Walter Scott, *Lay of the Last Minstrel*.

1806   Rhine Confederation established by Napoleon. Gabriel Legouvé, *Death of Henri IV*, performed in Paris.

1809   Austria concludes Peace of Vienna with France.

1810   Napoleon annexes Holland.

1811   Charles Stothard begins publication of *Monumental Effigies*.

1812   Napoleon begins retreat from Moscow. Prussia leads War of Liberation.

1814   Napoleon abdicates. Bourbon dynasty returns to France. Walter Scott, *Waverley*.

1815   Battle of Waterloo. Second Restoration of Bourbon dynasty.

1816   Alexandre Lenoir closes Musée des monuments français.

1818   Allied troops leave France.

1819   John Sell Cotman, *Architectural Antiquities of Normandy*, begins publication. François-Marius Granet exhibits *Choir of the Capuchin Church, Rome*.

1820   Assassination of the Duc de Berry in Paris. Washington Irving, *The Sketch Book*. First volume of *Voyages pittoresques et romantiques dans l'ancienne France*. Walter Scott, *Ivanhoe*.

1821   Death of Napoleon at St. Helena.

1822   Victor Hugo, *Odes*. Louis Daguerre opens diorama in Paris.

1823   François-René de Châteaubriand foreign minister of France.

1824   Death of Louis XVIII of France. Eugène Delacroix, *Massacre of Chios*. Prosper de Barante, *Histoire des Ducs de Bourgogne*. Leopold von Ranke, *History of the Latin and Teutonic Nations*.

1825   Coronation of Charles X at Reims. Augustin Thierry, *History of the Norman Conquest*.

1827   Victor Hugo, preface to *Cromwell*. Nicéphore Niepce, first photographic experiments. Exhibition at the Paris salon of Devéria, *Birth of Henri IV*. Eugène Delacroix, *Death of Sardanapalus*, and Paul Delaroche, *Death of Elizabeth, Queen of England*. Death of William Parkes Bonington.

1828   Thomas Babington Macaulay, essay "History." Prosper de Barante, essay "History."

1830   First showing of Victor Hugo's drama *Ernani*. July Revolution: abdication of Charles X and accession to the French throne of Louis-Philippe. Georg-Wilhelm-Friedrich Hegel, lectures on *The Philosophy of History*.

1832   Reform bill in England.

1833   Jules Michelet begins publication of *History of France*.

1834   Alexandre du Sommerard opens Musée de Cluny.

1837   Thomas Carlyle, *French Revolution*.

1838   Louis-Philippe begins redecoration of Château de Pau. Alexandre du Sommerard begins publication of *Les Arts au moyen âge*.

1839   Louis Daguerre announces invention of daguerreotype through French Academy of Sciences.

1843   Musée de Cluny acquired by the French state.

1848   Year of Revolution in Europe. Louis-Philippe abdicates.

1849   Thomas Babington Macaulay begins publication of *History of England*.

1850   Gilbert A'Beckett, *Comic History of England*.

1851   Opening of British Museum in its new building.

1852   Karl Marx, *Eighteenth Brumaire of Louis Bonaparte*.

1856   Alexis de Tocqueville, *The Ancien Régime and the Revolution*.

1859   Gustave Flaubert, *Salammbô*.

1860   Jacob Burckhardt, *Civilization of the Renaissance in Italy*.

1870   Franco-Prussian War. Abdication of Napoleon III.

1874   Friedrich Nietzsche, *Use and Abuse of History*.

1887   Pierre Loti inaugurates his "Salle gothique."

1895   Lord Acton, inaugural lecture on the study of history. Foundation of National Trust in Britain.

Notes and References

PREFACE

1. Lord Acton, *Lectures on Modern History* (London: Fontana, 1960), 36; hereafter cited in text as *LMH*.

2. Karl Marx, *The Eighteenth Brumaire of Louis Bonaparte* (Moscow: Progress, 1967), 8–9; hereafter cited in text as *EB*.

CHAPTER 1

1. Roy Porter and Mikulas Teich, eds., *Romanticism in National Context* (Cambridge: Cambridge University Press, 1988), 4; hereafter cited in text.

2. See Suzanne Gearhart, *The Open Boundary of History and Fiction* (Princeton: Princeton University Press, 1984).

3. See Harold Bloom, introduction to *Selected Writings of Walter Pater* (New York: Columbia University Press, 1982), xxxi.

4. For a useful collection of essays bearing on this theme, see H. Aram Veeser, ed., *The New Historicism* (London and New York: Routledge, 1989).

5. See Krishan Kumar, "The End of Socialism? The End of Utopia? The End of History?" in *Utopias and the Millennium*, ed. Krishan Kumar and Stephen Bann (London: Reaktion Books, 1993), 63–80.

6. See Patrick Wright, *On Living in an Old Country: The National Past in Contemporary Britain* (London: Verso, 1985), and Peter Vergo, ed., *The New Museology* (London: Reaktion, 1989), for a critical exploration of this issue.

7. Alois Riegl, "The Modern Cult of Monuments: Its Character and Its Origin," trans. Kurt W. Forster and Diane Ghirardo, *Oppositions* 25 (Fall 1982): 33; hereafter cited in text.

8. See Jean Piaget, "The Psychogenesis of Knowledge and Its Epistemological Significance," in *Language and Learning—The Debate between Jean Piaget and Noam Chomsky*, ed. Massimo Piattelli-Palmarini (London: Routledge, 1980), 34. Piaget's original view of cognitive development is summed up in his *Origins of Intelligence in Children* (New York: International Universities Press, 1966).

9. Eric Hobsbawm and Terence Ranger, eds., *The Invention of Tradition* (Cambridge: Cambridge University Press, 1983), 80; hereafter cited in text.

10. Prosper de Barante, *Histoire des Ducs de Bourgogne de la Maison de Valois*, 6th ed. (Paris: Furne, 1842), 1:xxii; hereafter cited in text as *HDB*.

11. Michel Foucault, *Les Mots et les choses* (Paris: Gallimard, 1966), 379. This text also exists in an English translation as *The Order of Things* (New York: Pantheon, 1971).

12. St. Augustine, *City of God*, ed. David Knowles (Harmondsworth: Penguin, 1988), 39–88.

13. It would be interesting to consider the "curiosity" for the past noted by Barante, and Foucault, in light of the earlier phenomenon defined by Krzysztof Pomian as exercising "an interim rule between those of theology and science." See Krzysztof Pomian, *Collectors and Curiosities* (Cambridge: Polity, 1990), 64.

CHAPTER 2

1. G. W. F. Hegel, *The Philosophy of History*, trans. J. Sibree (New York: Dover, 1956), 60.

2. Quoted from manuscript sources in Lionel Kochan, *Acton on History* (London: Deutsch, 1954), 60.

3. Albertine de Broglie, quoted in Prosper de Barante, *Souvenirs* (Paris, 1890–97), 3:248.

CHAPTER 3

1. See Philippa Levine, *The Amateur and the Professional: Antiquarians, Historians, and Archaeologists in Victorian England 1838–1886* (Cambridge: Cambridge University Press, 1986), 24.

2. See Roland Barthes, *Essais critiques* (Paris: Seuil, 1964), 124.

3. Quoted in Fritz Stern, ed., *The Varieties of History: From Voltaire to the Present* (London: Macmillan, 1970), 57; hereafter cited in text.

4. Quoted in Stephen Bann, *The Clothing of Clio: A Study of the*

Representation of History in Nineteenth-Century Britain and France (Cambridge: Cambridge University Press, 1984), 30; hereafter cited in text.

5. Prosper de Barante, *Etudes historiques et biographiques* (Paris: Didier, 1857), 2: 218; hereafter cited in text as *EHB*.

6. Augustin Thierry, *The Formation and Progress of the Tiers Etat*, trans. Rev. F. B. Wells (London: Bohn, 1859), 81.

7. Friedrich Nietzsche, *Human, All Too Human*, trans. R. J. Hollingdale (Cambridge: Cambridge University Press, 1986), 13; hereafter cited in text as *HAH*.

8. Friedrich Nietzsche, *The Use and Abuse of History*, trans. Adrian Collins (Indianapolis: Bobbs-Merrill, 1978), 12; hereafter cited in text as *UAH*.

CHAPTER 4

1. See David Lowenthal, *The Past Is a Foreign Country* (Cambridge: Cambridge University Press, 1985), 185. See "Changing the Past," 263–362.

2. Francis Haskell, *History and Its Images: Art and the Reinterpretation of the Past* (New Haven: Yale University Press, 1993), 236–77; hereafter cited in text.

3. Hayden White, *Metahistory: The Historical Imagination in Nineteenth-Century Europe* (Baltimore: Johns Hopkins University Press, 1973), 1–2; hereafter cited in text.

4. David Levin, *History as Romantic Art: Bancroft, Prescott, Motley and Parkman* (New York: AMS Press, 1967), ix.

5. Hayden White, *Tropics of Discourse: Essays in Cultural Criticism* (Baltimore: Johns Hopkins University Press, 1978), 110; hereafter cited in text.

6. Emile Benveniste, *Problèmes de linguistique générale* (Paris: Gallimard, 1966), 1:238–42; hereafter cited in text.

7. Roland Barthes, "The Discourse of History," trans. Stephen Bann, *Comparative Criticism* 3 (1981): 7; hereafter cited in text.

8. Roland Barthes, *Michelet*, trans. Richard Howard (Oxford: Blackwell, 1987), 96–7.

9. Roland Barthes, "The Reality Effect," trans. R. Carter, in *French Literary Theory Today*, ed. Tzvetan Todorov (Cambridge: Cambridge University Press, 1982), 15; hereafter cited in text.

CHAPTER 5

1. See René Lanson, *Le Goût du Moyen Age en France au XVIIIe siècle* (Paris: Vanoest, 1926), 5; hereafter cited in text.

2. See Gilbert Abbott A'Beckett, *The Comic History of England*,

with twenty colored etchings and two hundred woodcuts by John Leech (London: Bradbury, Evans and Co., 1851–52); hereafter cited in text.

3. See Bann 1984, 49–52, for a more extensive discussion of Michelet's treatment of the history of Joan of Arc.

4. Thomas de Quincey, *The English Mail Coach and Other Essays* (London: Everyman, 1970), 137; hereafter cited in text.

5. Jules Michelet, *Joan of Arc*, trans. Albert Guerard (Ann Arbor: University of Michigan Press, 1974), 48; hereafter cited in text.

6. See Marina Warner, "Personification and the Idealization of the Feminine," in *Medievalism in American Culture*, ed. Bernard Rosenthal and Paul E. Szarmach (Binghamton, N. Y.: Medieval and Renaissance Texts and Studies, 1989), 101–5.

7. Prosper de Barante, *Etudes littéraires et historiques* (Paris: Didier, 1858), 1:421.

CHAPTER 6

1. Victor Burgin, *The End of Art Theory* (London: Macmillan, 1986), 41.

2. Sigmund Freud, *New Introductory Lectures on Psychoanalysis* (Harmondsworth: Penguin, 1979), 94–95.

3. Sigmund Freud, *On Sexuality* (Harmondsworth: Penguin, 1977), 357; hereafter cited in text.

4. P. Anselme, *Histoire de la Maison Royale de France* (New York and London: Johnson, 1967), 1:146.

5. Robert Balland, *Sully—soldat, ministre, et gentilhomme campagnard 1560–1641* (Paris: Gamber, 1932), 81–82.

6. Bernard Barbiche, *Sully* (Paris: Albin Michel, 1978), 192. Details about Sully and his family have been taken from this source.

7. See Norman Bryson, *Word and Image: French Painting of the Ancien Regime* (Cambridge: Cambridge University Press, 1981), 204–8.

8. Patrick Noon, *Richard Parkes Bonington: On the Pleasure of Painting* (London and New Haven: Yale University Press, 1991), 230; hereafter cited in text.

CHAPTER 7

1. David Irwin, ed., *Winckelmann Writings on Art* (London: Phaidon, 1972), 137.

2. Johann-Wolfgang von Goethe, *Autobiography*, trans. R. O. Moon (London: Alston Rivers, 1932), 311; hereafter cited in text.

3. Quoted in Lorenz Eitner, ed., *Neoclassicism and Romanticism 1750–1850* (New York: Prentice Hall, 1971), 75–76.

4. See Nicholas Boyle, *Goethe: The Poet and the Age* (Oxford: Clarendon, 1991), 1:208; hereafter cited in text.

5. See the excellent analysis of Hugo's remark in Jeffrey Mehlman, *Revolution and Repetition: Marx/Hugo/Balzac* (Berkeley: University of California Press, 1977), 72–73.

6. See R. F. Jessup, "The Faussett Pavilion," *Archaeologia Cantiana* 66 (1953): 1–14; hereafter cited in text.

7. See J. G. Lockhart, *The Life of Sir Walter Scott* (London: Black, 1912), 810, for a useful listing of the various portraits of the novelist. Landseer's 1824 portrait, which features the lower half of the suit of armor featured by Watson Gordon, is discussed in Bann 1984, 68–70. (Lockhart's *Life* is hereafter cited in text as *LWS*.)

CHAPTER 8

1. "Un lifting seulement pour Notre-Dame," *Le Figaro*, 20 April 1993, 18.

2. See *Memoirs of the Painter Granet*, trans. Joseph Focarino, in *François-Marius Granet* catalogue (New York: Frick Collection, 1988), 36–38.

3. For an idea of the scale of this phenomenon, see Beth S. Wright and Paul Joannides, "Les romans historiques de Sir Walter Scott et la peinture française, 1822–1863," *Société de l'Histoire de l'Art français*, Bulletin 1982, 119–32. See also Wright, "Walter Scott et la gravure française," *Nouvelles de l'estampe* 93 (July 1987): 6–19, and "The Auld Alliance in Nineteenth-Century French Painting: The Changing Concept of Mary Stuart, 1814–1833," *Arts Magazine* 58, no. 7 (March 1984): 97–107.

4. Baronne de Barante, ed., *Lettres de Prosper de Barante à Mme de Staël* (Clermont-Ferrand: privately printed, 1929), 215.

5. See *Drop Gate, Duncombe Park* (1806) and *Chirk Aqueduct* (1806–1807), reproduced in *John Sell Cotman 1782–1842* catalogue (London: Arts Council of Great Britain, 1982), 74, 86–87, 105; hereafter cited in text as *Cotman*.

6. Charles Alfred Stothard, *Monumental Effigies* (London: 1811–33), 2 (passage quoted in Kempe's 1832 introduction). For further discussion of Stothard's achievement, see Bann 1984, 64–68.

7. John Sell Cotman, *Architectural Antiquities of Normandy Accompanied by Historical and Descriptive Notices by Dawson Turner* (London: 1822), 4, 107; hereafter cited in text as *Normandy*.

8. See Adele M. Holcomb, *John Sell Cotman* (London: British Museum, 1978), 14.

9. Hubert Damisch, *L'Origine de la perspective* (Paris: Flammarion, 1987), 62.

10. See Umberto Eco, "A Reading of *Steve Canyon*," *20th Century Studies* 13/14 (1976): 14–33.

11. Quoted in *Le Gothique retrouvé*, catalogue (Paris: Caisse Nationale des monuments historiques et des sites, 1979), 107–9.

12. Harry Ransom Humanities Research Center, University of Texas at Austin, Gernsheim Collection, listed under Daguerre.

13. See Roland Barthes, *La Chambre claire* (Paris: Seuil, 1980), 146, for this distinction.

14. See Izaak Walton, *The Complete Angler*, facsimile repr. of 1st ed. (London: Elliott Stock, c. 1880), ix.

CHAPTER 9

1. Report in *Independent*, 17 August 1993, 1.

2. Niccolò Machiavelli, *Opere scelte*, ed. Gian Franco Berardi (Rome: Editori Riuniti, 1969), 596.

3. See J. E. Law and Martin Davies, "What Did Machiavelli Wear in the Country?" *Bulletin of the Society for Renaissance Studies* 1, no. 2 (May 1983): 12–18. For a further discussion of the variant forms of the text see Cecil H. Clough, "Machiavelli's 'Epistolario' and Again What Did Machiavelli Wear in the Country," *Bulletin of the Society for Renaissance Studies*, 1, no. 3 (October 1983): 7–18. I am grateful to my colleague Dr. Diego Zancani for drawing my attention to this debate.

4. See *Portrait présumé de Henri IV enfant*, Collection Musée National du Château de Pau, P. 84. 10. 1.

5. The objects referred to are exhibited in the Grand Salon de Reception, Château de Pau.

6. Unsigned review in *Le Publiciste*, 27 June 1806, feuilleton.

7. Stendhal (H. Beyle), *Racine et Shakspeare* (Paris, 1854), 35–36.

8. See *De David à Delacroix: La peinture française de 1774 à 1830*, catalogue (Paris: Editions des Musées Nationaux, 1974), 394. There are large-scale versions of the work in the collections of the Louvre and of the City of Pau.

9. See Marie-Claude Chaudonneret, "Historicism and 'Heritage' in the Louvre 1820–40: From the Musée Charles X to the Galerie d'Apollon," *Art History* 14, no. 4 (December 1991): 489.

10. For a fuller discussion of the Musée de Cluny, see Bann 1984, 77–92, and Stephen Bann, *The Inventions of History: Essays on the Representation of the Past* (Manchester: Manchester University Press, 1990), 122–47.

11. Mme. de Saint-Surin, *L'Hôtel de Cluny au Moyen Age* (Paris, 1835); hereafter cited in text. I am glad to acknowledge that my attention

was drawn to the existence of this very useful source by Sarah Kane's M.A. dissertation (Courtauld Institute, 1993) on the Musée de Cluny.

12. *The Canterbury Tales*, publicity leaflet produced by Canterbury City Council.

13. Emile Deschamps, "Visite à l'hôtel de Cluny," in *Notice sur l'Hôtel de Cluny et sur le Palais des Thermes* (Paris, December 1834), 234.

14. See Tzvetan Todorov, "The Fantastic in Fiction," *20th Century Studies* 3 (May 1970): 76–92.

15. Umberto Eco, *Travels in Hyperreality* (London: Picador, 1987), 67.

16. See Marie-Pascale Bault, *Le dîner Louis XI de Pierre Loti*, exhibition catalogue (Rochefort-sur-mer: Maison de Pierre Loti, 30 June–23 October 1988); hereafter cited in text.

17. See Robert Laube, ". . . und Waffen uns an treuesten Verbrudern," in *Vergessenen Zeiten: Mittelalter in Ruhrgebiet*, catalogue (Essen: Ruhrlandmuseum, September 1990–January 1991), 2: 329–36.

18. Frank Barrett, "Fit for a King, or a Millionaire," *Independent*, 28 August 1993, 44; hereafter cited in text.

19. *Castle Drogo, Devon* (London: National Trust 1992), 5; cited hereafter in text as *Drogo*.

CONCLUSION

1. See Louis Marin, *Des pouvoirs de l'image* (Paris: Seuil, 1993), 9–22.

2. See Stephen Bann, "Generating the Renaissance, or the Individualization of Culture," in *The Point of Theory*, ed. Mieke Bal and Inge Boer (Amsterdam: University of Amsterdam Press, 1994), 145–54.

Bibliographic Essay

In the foregoing study, I have attempted to interpret the historical-mindedness of the Romantic epoch in a new way, insisting on the relevance of the concepts of representation and discourse, while at the same time exemplifying their analytic potential through the use of a sequence of visual examples. This is not, however, a contribution to art history in the accepted sense but rather an instance of the way in which cultural history in the broadest sense of the term may be illuminated by a close attention to the signifying features of the image. Here it is not simply a question of "illustrating" the argument but of utilizing the special features of visual communication to set up a dialogue between the present-day consciousness of history and the creation of new codes of historical awareness that, according to my contention, were established in the course of the nineteenth century.

Being defined in this way, the project touches on a number of important, and largely self-contained, fields of inquiry, such as history of historiography, philosophy of history, and history of art, without being precisely coincident with any of them. My suggestions for further reading will therefore be limited, on the whole, to works that set up a specific argument about the context and significance of the nineteenth-century cult of history and relate it in some way to the issues of our own period.

Two important contemporary studies that reflect opposing attitudes to the subject (neither of them directly related to my own) may be mentioned first. In *The Past Is a Foreign Country* (Cambridge: Cambridge

179

University Press, 1985), David Lowenthal resourcefully manipulates a mass of evidence, both textual and visual, under broad general categories: "Wanting the Past," "Knowing the Past," and "Changing the Past." It is obvious how closely my own approach adheres to this basic pattern, in taking as its first premise the heterogeneity of possible attitudes to the past. Nonetheless, Lowenthal is basically concerned with classifying and analyzing the phenomena of historical awareness from an anthropological point of view, and he is for that reason not specifically concerned with the genesis of "historical-mindedness" on a historical level.

By contrast, Francis Haskell's *History and Its Images* (New Haven and London: Yale University Press, 1993) addresses the specific and fascinating issue of the historian's use of the image for evidence. It therefore takes for granted the analytic skills developed by the nineteenth-century historian and shows how inadequate they have ultimately proved to be in the elucidation of the status of the image as a form of historical evidence. Haskell's chapters "The Musée des Monuments Français," "Michelet," and "The Historical Significance of Style" (referring to Ruskin, Burckhardt, and Taine) are specially valuable as indications of the creative powers of the nineteenth-century pioneers.

The theorist who most sharply defines the break with nineteenth-century historiography in terms of method, and thus sets the stage for a more radical critical approach to the phenomenon of historical consciousness, is of course Michel Foucault. In this particular domain, his fundamental texts are *The Order of Things*, trans. Alan Sheridan (London: Tavistock and New York: Pantheon, 1970), and *The Archaeology of Knowledge*, trans. Alan Sheridan (London: Tavistock and New York: Pantheon, 1972). There is a good account of his work as a whole, together with a preliminary bibliography, in Alan Sheridan, *Michel Foucault: The Will to Truth* (London and New York: Tavistock, 1980).

If Foucault is profoundly imbued with the spirit of nineteenth-century historical analysis—and particularly that of Marx and Nietzsche—Roland Barthes is the first critic and theorist to assess the full importance of the concept of representation in elucidating examples from the period. His *Michelet*, trans. Richard Howard (New York: Farrar, Straus and Giroux, 1987) is a virtuoso celebration of the Romantic historian par excellence. Among the many essays in which he deals, sometimes uproariously, with historical material, it is impossible to exclude "The Discourse of History," trans. Stephen Bann, *Comparative Criticism: A Yearbook* 3 (1981), and "The Reality Effect," trans. R. Carter, in *French Literary Theory Today: A Reader*, ed. Tzvetan Todorov (Cambridge and New York: Cambridge University Press, 1982).

In the Anglo-American context, by far the most important stimulus to the revision of views about the historical consciousness of the nineteenth century has come from the work of Hayden White, beginning with *Metahistory: The Historical Imagination in Nineteenth-Century Europe* (Baltimore: Johns Hopkins University Press, 1973). Two subsequent collections of essays have extended and broadened his inquiry into the conditions of historical-mindedness: *Tropics of Discourse: Essays in Cultural Criticism* (Baltimore: Johns Hopkins University Press, 1978) and *The Content of the Form: Narrative Discourse and Historical Representation* (Baltimore: Johns Hopkins University Press, 1987).

Among the other valuable metahistorical studies that have been published over the last twenty years, it is necessary to mention one of the first attempts to examine the figural logic of a Romantic historian: Lionel Gossman's *Augustin Thierry and Liberal Historiography, History and Theory*, Beiheft 15 (Middletown, Conn.: Wesleyan University Press, 1976). Gossman's essay "History and Literature: Reproduction or Signification?" is one of a number of excellent essays in Robert H. Canary and Henry Kozicki, eds., *The Writing of History: Literary Form and Historical Understanding* (Madison: University of Wisconsin Press, 1978), which includes valuable "suggestions for further reading."

Anticipating my own central emphasis on French historical culture, there are a number of fine studies of the constitution of historical discourses during the postrevolutionary years. Linda Orr has published *Jules Michelet: Nature, History, and Language* (Ithaca: Cornell University Press, 1976) and *Headless History: Nineteenth-Century French Historiography of the Revolution* (Ithaca: Cornell University Press, 1990). Ann Rigney has made a comparative analysis of the histories of Lamartine, Michelet, and Louis Blanc in *The Rhetoric of Historical Representation: Three Narrative Histories of the French Revolution* (Cambridge and New York: Cambridge University Press, 1990).

Differing perspectives on the value of the new metahistorical approach, not all of them favorable, can be found in *The Representation of Historical Events, History and Theory*, Beiheft 26 (Middletown, Conn.: Wesleyan University Press, 1987). Contributors to the debate carried on over the years in the journal *History and Theory* include F. R. Ankersmit and Hans Kellner, who have recently edited the collection of essays *A New Philosophy of History* (London: Reaktion Books, 1994), which reflects in part the new emphasis on visual materials in analyzing historical culture. Ankersmit is also the author of *Narrative Logic: A Semantic Analysis of the Historian's Language* (The Hague: Mouton, 1983) and Kellner of *Language and Historical Representation: Getting the Story Crooked* (Madison: University of Wisconsin Press, 1989).

Other useful works that reflect the continuing reappraisal of the professionalized historiography of the nineteenth century include Philippa Levine's absorbing study, *The Amateur and the Professional: Antiquarians, Historians and Archaeologists in Victorian England 1838-1886* (Cambridge and New York: Cambridge University Press, 1986). This provides much of the essential data for a conceptual distinction between the different types of professional concern with the past comparable to that which was developed for collectors and connoisseurs in the preceding period by Krzysztof Pomian, *Collectors and Curiosities*, trans. Elizabeth Wiles-Porter (Oxford: Polity Press, 1990). As yet, however, it is not easy to find works that treat the phenomenon of antiquarianism with an adequate seriousness. Stuart Piggott's *William Stukeley: An Eighteenth-Century Antiquary*, rev. and enl. ed. (London: Thames and Hudson, 1985), is a valuable exception.

Art history has been slow to focus on the issue of historical representation as one deserving of special attention. There are, however, a number of valuable catalogues that provide repertoires of images, as well as texts that offer special insights into the processes of representing the past in relation to the constraints of style and medium. For French painting over the relevant period, there is a wealth of documentation to be found in the catalogue *De David à Delacroix: La peinture française de 1774 à 1830* (Paris: Editions des Musées Nationaux, 1974), which contains two essays by Robert Rosenblum on the period from the Consulate to the Restoration. Another catalogue, *Le "Gothique" retrouvé avant Viollet-le-Duc* (Paris: Caisse Nationale des Monuments historiques et des Sites, 1979), ranges widely through British and German materials while being essentially based in the historical culture of France. Patrick Noon's *Richard Parkes Bonington: On the Pleasure of Painting* (New Haven: Yale Center for British Art, 1991) is a catalogue worthy of its subject matter, which shows the full range of Bonington's virtuosity and examines it thoughtfully. Edward Morris and Frank Milner's *And When Did You Last See Your Father?* (Liverpool: Walker Art Gallery, 1992) approaches historical genre painting from the other end of the century and has interesting things to say about the links between painting and forms of popular spectacle, like waxworks.

Insofar as this study is about the critical reappraisal of the status of "history" within a whole range of contemporary cultural practices, it could lead to more specialized coverage of a great number of different fields. One would obviously be the field of literary history, where the "New Historicism" has already attracted much comment and is the subject of a useful anthology containing many different views: H. Aram Veeser, ed., *The New Historicism* (New York: Routledge, 1989). Another would be art history itself, whose genealogy has been skillfully, if idiosyncratically, deconstructed by Donald Preziosi in *Rethinking Art History: Meditations on a Coy Science* (New Haven and London: Yale University Press, 1989). Perhaps most symptomatic of the historical reflection to which I have attempted to contribute is the contemporary burgeoning of "museology" as a subject of study. Peter Vergo, ed., *The New Museology* (London: Reaktion Books, 1989), is a good conspectus of the questions raised by this particular mode of constructing the past. Eilean Hooper-Greenhill's *Museums and the Shaping of Knowledge* (New York and London: Routledge, 1992) is a solid, if slightly severe, discussion, much influenced by Foucault, while Umberto Eco, in *Travels in Hyper-Reality*, trans. William Weaver (New York: Harcourt, Brace, Jovanovich, 1986), delightfully presents the flip side.

Index

The Author

STEPHEN BANN was born in Manchester, United Kingdom, in 1942 and educated at Winchester College and King's College, Cambridge, where he gained a Double First Class degree in the History Tripos, and subsequently took his Ph.D. in 1967. From that date, he has taught at the University of Kent at Canterbury, where he is now professor and director of the Centre of Modern Cultural Studies, as well as being chair of the Board of Studies in History and Theory of Art. His publications over the past ten years include *The Clothing of Clio* (1984), *The True Vine* (1989), *The Inventions of History* (1990), and *Under the Sign: John Bargrave as Traveler, Collector, and Witness* (1994). He has also coedited *Interpreting Contemporary Art* (1991) and *Utopias and the Millennium* (1993) and translated Julia Kristeva's *Proust and the Sense of Time* (1993). He has held numerous visiting appointments at universities outside Britain, notably in France and the United States, and has contributed to a wide range of international journals and publications in the areas of history of historiography, art theory, and cultural criticism.